THE LINTON PORCUPINE

THE
LINTON
PORCUPINE

*Transcribed and translated
into modern English
by*

Ross Laidlaw

CANONGATE
1984

First published in 1984
by Canongate Publishing Ltd, Edinburgh

ISBN 0 86241 063 0

*The publishers acknowledge the financial assistance
of the Scottish Arts Council in the
publication of this volume*

The jacket illustration is from Henry VIII's psalter,
Royal M.S. reproduced by kind permission of the
British Library.

To Simon, Alyn and Margaret

Typeset by Witwell Ltd, Liverpool
Printed by Oxford University Press

CONTENTS

TRANSCRIBER'S NOTE

In December 1982, a friend in the course of sorting through family archives, came across a bundle of papers which he thought might be of historical interest. Knowing that I had been an archivist, he passed them on to me for my comments.

The bundle proved to be a manuscript journal, written up from notes taken 'in the field' in 1545, by one Nicholas Wainwright. In the course of transcription, it emerged that Wainwright was an English spy sent on a special mission to Scotland by Henry VIII's Secretary of State. The mission's objective was to find and destroy the 'Porcupine' — a secret engine of war which the Scots were in the process of developing. As a primary source throwing new light on technology and Anglo-Scottish relations in the mid-sixteenth century, the document seems as though it might prove to be an exciting and significant discovery. (See Appendices.)

I couldn't help wondering what Wainwright's thoughts might be if he could somehow be transported to the present and revisit the places which he describes in his account. Much he would find changed, some of it swept away utterly, some altered beyond recognition. But a surprising amount would be familiar. The Kings' School, Ely (and of course the Cathedral) survives miraculously preserved almost as it was in Wainwright's day. (In the upper storey of Prior Crauden's Chapel, you will find if you look carefully, the carved initials 'N W' on a pillar on the right as you face the altar.) Much of Cambridge still wears the same general aspect that it did when Wainwright went up, but he would find his own College — Gonville Hall, refounded and largely rebuilt by his old mentor Dr. Caius.

In today's vast sprawling metropolis, he would have difficulty at first in recognising anything of the picturesque little London that he knew. He would soon however discover familiar landmarks — Westminster Abbey (having sprouted its Wren towers in the interim), St. Mary Overy (now Southwark Cathedral), and of course the Tower. Also the street plan and many place-names of the City and its environs would be recognizable.

In the Lothians, the noble bones of the landscape — the Lammermuirs, the Pentlands, Arthur's Seat, the Laws of North Berwick and Traprain (which he knew as Dunpender), overlook a scenery more cultivated and populous than in his day but not so very different in essentials, if one discounts the ravages of war. The little towns, more extensive now, are still there and he would see many familiar landmarks. At East Linton — plain Linton in 1545, the bridge is the one that he knew (and which Somerset's army was to cross two years later) and the Curling Club, founded just seven years before Wainwright arrived in Linton, still flourishes. Preston Mill is one o the few working water-mills left in the country, and the great beehive of Phantassie Doocot looms above the cornfields as solid as ever.

The massive keep of Lethington (now Lennoxlove) must look from the outside much as it did to Wainwright, and he would recognize parts of the interior. The years have been less kind to Garleton Castle but he would find quite a lot of it intact — including perhaps the room where he spoke with Sir David Lindsay. He might shudder to find the pit prison in Hailes Castle unaltered since his tenancy of it, but he would probably derive a wry satisfaction from the marks caused by the conflagration which he started, still visible on the walls of the Chapel (and ascribed erroneously in the Department of the Environment's leaflet to an earlier fire of 1532).

In Edinburgh's Old Town, he would find his way with ease among the streets and wynds, their position largely unaltered since his day, although the buildings themselves have been rebuilt for the most part — a notable exception being the house of John Mossman (known today as John Knox's House*). And he might be surprised to find that the 'guid Scots tongue' which Ascham so deplored, and whose imminent demise he predicted (along with pundits in every century since) survives, despite everything that four hundred odd years of official, social and cultural opposition has found to throw at it.

He would certainly find similarities between the striving, increasingly materialistic values of his own (and Machiavelli's) world and ours, and he might well note, with a frisson of recognition, some striking parallels between international politics of the mid-sixteenth and late twentieth centuries. In some ways, Wainwright's world is closer to our own, than we are to those of the intervening centuries. His world was still that of the Renaissance rather than the Reformation, when men looked about them with fresh enquiring minds, and lived life with a gusto and directness uninhibited by the sort of social complexes and compulsions that were to develop in the course of the next three centuries, and from which we are only now beginning to extricate ourselves — Calvinism, the Work Ethic, Race Prejudice, Imperialism, Victorian sexual hang-ups, and so forth. Wainwright would probably find a meeting with any of the following, heavy going — Bunyan, Wesley, Ruskin, Dr. Arnold, or even John Buchan. But he might well establish an immediate rapport with Billy Conolly or Dorothy Dunnet.

Regarding Wainwright's M.S., after transcribing it as it stands, I decided to 'translate' it into modern colloquial English. The average reader would be able to understand the text of the original with little difficulty — so why bother? I did so for the following reasons.

Wainwright's English is pithy and direct and conveys a sense of immediacy; almost, he seems to grab you by the lapel and compel your attention. His cast of mind and attitude to circumstances seem in many ways astonishingly modern (for example his flippant humour, keen perception of what 'makes people tick', lack of reverence for 'Sacred Cows', and a certain wry awareness of his own shortcomings) — it is almost as if a contemporary were speaking to us across a gulf of four and a half centuries. This quality of modernity would, I thought, be obscured to some extent if the reader could only receive the sense of Wainwright's words through a filter of unfamiliar or archaic language. Perhaps this is presumption on my part; my justification must be that I tried to give his words the sort of ring for us, that they would have had for his contemporaries of 1545. A comparison of the transcription of the Introduction, with my own 'translation' into modern English of the remainder of the text, will give some indication as to how far I have been successful — or otherwise.

Wainwright's M.S. is written as a single unbroken narrative. In deference to modern taste, I have taken the liberty of breaking it up into parts, where the breaks seemed natural. I have given these parts my own invented headings, suggested by a main event occurring in each.

R.L.

*The Reformer may have rented the house from John Mossman's son James, in the 1560's, although the evidence for this seems somewhat tenuous.

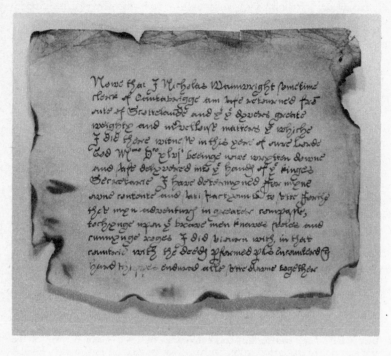

Transcription of part of the first page of
Nicholas Wainwright's M.S.

INTRODUCTION

Nowe that I Nicholas Waiwright sometime clerk of Cantabrigge am safe retourned from oute of Scottelaunde and that the dyvers greate weighty and marvellouse matters the whiche I did there witnesse in this yere of oure Lorde God 1545 beeinge nowe wrytten downe and safe delyvered into the handes of the kinges Secretarie I have determyned For myne owne contente and satisfactyoun to sette Forthe these myne adventures in greater compasse, tochynge upon the brave men knaves fooles and cunnynge roges I did sojourn with in that countrie with the deedes performed perils encounterd & hardshippes endured all sette downe together with sundrie dyvers matters pertaynynge thereuntoe.

But to speake trulie (tho I saye it unto myselfe privilie) it woulde please me were this historie to be imprinted upon a daye. Roger Ascham that goode fellowe and honeste Yorkshireman would deem it recompense enow to have done goode servyce for the Kynge in furtheraunce of the comon welthe, yet have I suffered suche paynes affrytes and miseries unspeakable that I hazard there be noe man who having endured the like would not wish to speake thereof sumwhat unto his fellowes in especiall had he been thinstrumente by the whiche the realme was made secure (as the Kinges Secretarie hath sayde: I doe not saye this for myself lest I be thought vaynegloriouse).

If so there be anie that doe reade these wordes of myn unto hym woulde I saye ave lector, I shall telle you a lytel concernynge myselfe that you maye the better understaunde the causes of myn actes and policies related in this historie. I was borne in Ely in Cambridgeshyre in the fourteenthe yere of the rayne of the eighthe Henrie (who yet rayneth). My father followed the trade of merchandise (beinge generallie allowed thereby to be a gentilman tho lackynge cote armour) traffyckynge with merchauntes of the greater sort at one tyme at another with petty traders bodgeres and cadgers for the provisyonynge of suche thynges as those who lacked them myghte requeste, in especiall the munkes of Ely priorie (afore that the monasterys were suppressed) they practysynge but lytel husbandrie by cause of the fennie swampes encompassynge the Isle of Ely being lytel draynt, and soe they must needs obtayn their provisyonynge from other partes. When I was but a lytel chylde my mother died but after the passage of a fewe yeares mo my father wed agayne, hys seconde wyf a Juno to beholde but in her nature a verie shrewe that kept me at my hornebooke with many strypes to lern my ABC. When a chylde I stoode in myghtie dred of her but nowe in lyke maner as Kynge Codpiece hath supplanted Kynge Coates so Lewde Ymagynynge hath cast oute Fere[1] (more I dare not yet assaye for that woulde be unlawful and mortal sin to boote).

When I was eighte yeres olde I began my schoolynge at Ely priorie: (you shoulde knowe that the schoole whyche is called Schola Regia ought rather to be Schola Regum by these causes, Kynge Edwarde yclept[2] Confessor was a scoler there and oure Kynge Henrie hath these foure yeres past graunted a charter untoe the same). My beginnynge there was afore the suppressynge of the monasterys: I had wished oure Kynge had bethought hymselfe sooner of suche a cunnynge devyce to augmente hys purse for then mighte I have been spared verie mennie wearie houres of munkyshe mumblynge cherelesse chauntynge and woeful wailynge in Ely quyre under the rule of that puffed up tyraunte Christopher Tye (nowe master of the Choristeres at Ely but then a laye clarke in Kinges Colledge at Cambridge and who would oft tymes ryde to Ely). Yet when thaccompte be whollie reckoned up a scolers yoke there galled not overly an ye but exercised diligence and mother wit enow, nor lacked we for encoragemente; our kindlie Masters[3] of their goodwill neglected not to ayde us in thaccomplysshynge of oure taskes with strypes aplentie to thende that we be soundlie schooled (or as some woulde saye had Lilys Latin Grammare conned by rote).

Untoe Cambridge (beeinge the older and more famouse Universitie and but a dayes journey from Elie) in my sixteenth yere I went

---

[1] Long coats were worn by small children; 'breeching' — when a boy exchanged his coats for an adult style of dress, was something of an occasion, rather like the changeover from shorts to long trousers in our own time. It is interesting that Wainwright uses the imagery of characters in a Morality Play.

[2] yclept — called, named.

[3] They were Ralphe Holland and William Theolas; they seem to have been retained in their office after the Dissolution.

somethynge puffed up with vayne sillie fantasies[1] of becoming a lerned doctor. My fathers hope it was I sholde enter into Jesus Colledge (which was establyshed by Bisschope Alcock of Elie while my sire was yet in long cotes). This wolde have been a matter not difficile of bringing to pass my father being in the favour of My Lord Bysshope of Elie Doctor Goodrich a puissant prelate who could make smoothe the waye. But I being surfeyted with orisons and akynge knees (and the writ of oure Mother the Churche runnynge myghtie strong in Alcockes Colledge) did kick agaynst the prickes. Sore was the strife and long betwixt myself and my familie (choler did painte my stepmotheres cheeke and cause her eyen to glister that she seemed a verie Venus I recalle) but I prevayled at the laste and entered into Gonville Hall (an ancient Colledge yet froward in just lerninge) a sizar than which estate there be none lowlier for ye must needes serve as scullion in the kitchens and servitor to scolers with purses fatter than your owne, that ye may purchase your commons and battels withal.

But where was the famouse Newe Lerninge of the whiche (since even afore the time great Desiderius[2] of recent memorie sojourned there) men averred Cambridge to be the verie fons et origo and whiche I supposed had clean overthrowne the Scholemen of old tyme to wit Aquinas Duns the Scotte and their menie?[3] Marry as to that ye could have gulled me for I saw but scante shewinge thereof; the curriculum studiorum to become firstlie Bachelor then Master of Artes (whereof thaccomplysshinge was not afore the passage of seven yeres) was but the old Trivium and Quadrivium taken asunder then peeced together agayne (as a man mighte dismember his house then build it up anewe, noe matter that the forme thereof be changed the brickes and beames be yet the same). I had sufficiencie of wit and aptnesse to lern that I needed not to studie too sore in sad[4] lookynge upon my bokes so that what tyme my taskes in scolering and sizaring were accomplished, I woulde repayre untoe the Whyte Horse or the Falcone in Pettie Curie there to make good chere with wenches of the towne (which was a

---

[1] fantasies — fancies.
[2] i.e. Desiderius Erasmus.
[3] menie —following (literally household).
[4] sad — serious, earnest.

greate offence for a scoler with sore penalties an it were discovered).

During my time at Schola Regia in Elie priorie I had been passing famous among my fellowes for aping of our scholemaster and usher[1]. *My aptnesse herein I did nowe begin diligentlie to practyse and make perfite by cause of this right pleasaunte discoverie; when making merie with my fellowes at the ale, did I but make them sport by aping of the speeche and maners of dyvers greate notable doctors of the Universitie, then coulde I drincke my fille without ever loosing purse stringes. And nowe to make up the tale*[2] *of myn accomplysshmentes (by cause it hath beringe upon my historie hereafter as ye shall presentlie discover and not for noe desyre of vauntynge of myselfe) I shall add but this; I am of a goodlie lengthe well made and cumlye enow wythal (as sundrie damsels have been pleased to telle me) and can singe and playe to a gitteron*[3] *(that I had of a merchaunte was in Spayne).*

Thus passed I my life and tyme in Cambridge from daye to daye and yere to yere in such good chere and dallyaunce mirthe and pleasure (nothinge disposed to travayle in dustie bokes and ynkehorne[4] *scriblynges) yet tyllynge in Lerninges feelde enow (tho barely enow I graunte you) as to entertayne some juste hope of repynge the harveste thereof and beeinge made Master of Artes in this yere of oure Lorde God 1545; until Fortune began to wax somethynge wroth with the prosperous estate of Master Nicholas Wainwright Bachelor of Artes and to boote mynstrel scoler (which office I did holde but in commendam*[5] *my fellowes woulde of a suretie aver) Foole and lover; wherefore she procured Vayne follie to be her instrumente for thencompassynge (with a swifte and horrid sodaynenesse) of myn utter ruine and downefalle...*

[1] *or, as we would say — Head Master and Assistant Master.*

[2] *make up the tale — complete the tally.*

[3] *In view of the Spanish connection, some kind of guitar rather than a gittern proper, is probably meant.*

[4] *inkhorn — a term of derision applied to affectedly archaic or pedantic expressions by writers.*

[5] *in commendam — in trust or keeping. This phrase was used when benefices were given to persons who enjoyed their revenue without performing the duties attached to them.*

*The Journal of the Adventures of
Nicholas Wainwright, Clerk of Gonville Hall in the
University of Cambridge, and written by him in
the Year 1545.*

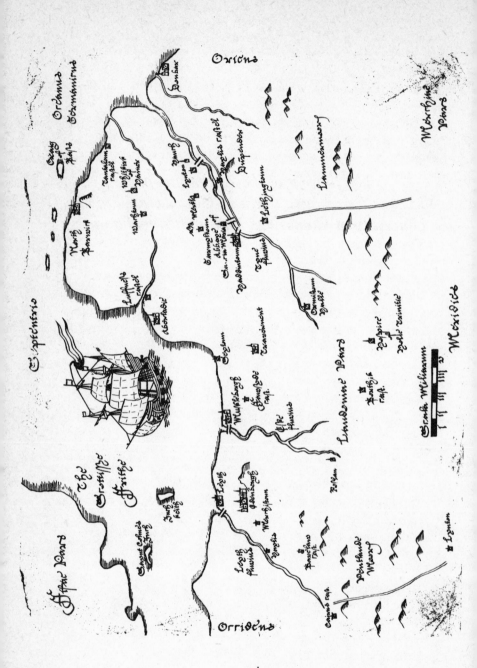

xiv

A NIGHT AT THE GARTER

.... SHORTLY BEFORE the start of the Summer Term, my father caught a severe chill as he was about to set off on a business trip to Slough, Bucks. A fever developed and my stepmother packed him off to bed. (In the Fens, such things can't be taken lightly.) I was deputed to go in his place, the rule that students should reside in College during the vacs having been waived in my case, my home being so close. I was not madly keen on the idea; the roads in those parts, besides being muddy from April showers were rumoured to be infested with sturdy beggars. These seemed to increase yearly as a result of unemployment stemming from enclosures, inflation and the shutting-down of the monasteries. But there was no help for it; since losing his best customer with the Dissolution, my father had to scratch for business wherever he could find it. I kissed my stepmother goodbye — a warm, lingering kiss that almost got me my ears boxed, then trotted off, breaking my journey that night at Dunstable. Next day, after running the gauntlet of some Palliards — con-merchants who cover themselves in fake sores, I reached Slough, mired to the crotch and with incipient saddle-sores from being out of practice.

By the following afternoon, the business (concerning consignments of beech timber) was settled. I could have reached Dunstable the same night, but I felt I had earned a respite; besides, the two red discs on my buttocks would rub raw unless rested. The supplier put me up willingly and next morning, dressed in a change of clothing from my saddlebag, I walked to Windsor, crossing the bridge below Eton College (about whose ex-head — 'Flogging Nick' Udall recently sacked for perversion with two of his pupils and connivance at their pinching college silver, horror-stories were circulated by undergrads at King's).

I sipped my second quart at the Garter appreciatively, deciding that the new hop-flavoured beverage from Germany — beer, was

1

infinitely preferable to the muddy ale served up in most English pubs. My chatting-up of the serving-girl had begun to progress nicely, when a noise outside attracted my attention. Looking out of the window, I saw people streaming past in a hurry. I downed my beer, patted the girl's hand and joining the crowd outside followed them down to the Thames.

A stirring din — trombones, cornets, crumhorns, blasted my ear drums, then from round a bend, downstream, swept a procession of barges, their oars rising and falling in unison. They were filled with courtiers and attendants — like so many tubs crammed with brightly-coloured flowers. On a dais in one craft, whose oarsmen sported the green and white Tudor livery, surrounded by scarlet-clad halberdiers towered a resplendent figure — a huge man, blazing in cloth-of-gold like an enormous sunflower.

I had never before seen our monarch, but that vast mound of gold-swathed flesh, which seemed to radiate a kind of baleful charisma, could be none other. (And of course, everyone was familiar with his appearance from hearsay and from the frontispiece of the Great Bible which had recently appeared in every church.) Pink and smooth as a great ham, the royal visage beamed at his subjects thronging the banks, and a pudgy hand encrusted with glittering rings, lifted in acknowledgement of their shouts of 'Long Live the King!' and 'God bless King Harry!' I felt a kind of empathy flow between the spectators and the Royal barge, and experienced a flash of insight into the source of Henry's power; if you stood high in the land better watch your neck, but between King and common people there existed a mutual regard and understanding.

The crowd in the Garter roared for an encore and another free pint was plonked down in front of me. I demolished the pint, and disengaging my arm from the waist of the serving girl, got up and placed my joint-stool on the table. I then proceeded, rather unsteadily, to clamber up onto the table and sit on the stool. My precarious perch metamorphosed into the dais on the royal barge .... I was Henry, the eighth of that name. The sweaty roisterers below me fell silent as my kingly gaze swept round the taproom — my loyal, loving subjects. Slowly, my beringed hand lifted in acknowledgement of their obeisance....

I climbed down to a storm of clapping and stamping. "Bravo! bravo! ... that was King Harry to the life ... how about doing us the Earl of Surrey..."

Further turns would have to wait for I was becoming uncomfortably aware of a pressing need to relieve myself. I weaved through the crowd and pushing through the door at the back blundered my way in the darkness to the outside privy.

I retied my codpiece point and left the privy, to be confronted by two men, dimly visable in the taper-light issuing from the rear windows of the pub. One was short, with sharp intelligent features and wearing a drab, but expensively-furred gown. The other, a great ox of a fellow with long, drooping moustaches, wore soiled and curiously old-fashioned finery — striped hose, tunic scalloped low in the neck, and an immense cap-plume.

"I say — that was *very* good," said Fox-face, laying a hand on my sleeve.

"Ja, verry goot," echoed Striped-pants in a sepulchral rumble. The accent was Germanic.

Fox-face held up a purse and swung it so that the contents chinked. "Perhaps we could talk somewhere," he murmured. He tapped the side of his nose and winked. "You know — ah, confidential."

"Convidensial," intoned Striped-pants.

The situation was so ludicrous that I almost laughed in their faces. But that was gold in the purse, or I was a Dutchman — and hard cash is never a laughing matter where N.Wainwright is concerned. Wondering muzzily what this pair of comedians' game was, but deciding there was nothing to lose, I replied breezily, "Lead on."

Seconds later we were ensconced in a private parlour, with a jug of Burgundy beside the candlesticks on the table.

"A remarkable performance," enthused Fox-face, pouring. He raised his tin cup. "Congratulations. Ever thought of turning professional?"

Again the urge to laugh swept over me. Was this clown serious? My M.A. when I got it, would be a licence to teach — hardly a

3

passport to riches, but compared to the life of a strolling player which is all my gift for mimicry would fit me for, wealth and security indeed.

"I'm listening," I said ignoring the question and wondering when he was going to get to the point.

"And to think we were in Windsor hunting for mere Reformers," went on Fox-face conversationally. "Rounded up a whole nest of them recently. Tiresome types — insist on interpreting Scripture for themselves, which is absolutely against the Six Articles, which I'm sure you know. Marbeck got off — Queen Catherine liked his singing unfortunately. But the rest fried at Smithfield." He grinned at me and chuckled, "Now you wouldn't be a Reformer by any chance?"

"Good God — no!" I exclaimed, a thread of unease twisting in my stomach. The comic aspect of the situation had suddenly evaporated.

"Excellent Burgundy don't you think," went on Fox-face. "Here, have some more." Wine splashed into my cup. "A Reformer — no, you're not the type." Then the mask of affability was whipped away and he spat out in tones of icy menace, "Treason's more your line, isn't it?"

"Treasson,"rumbled Striped-pants, nodding his head.

Treason. The word hung in the air like the echoes of a thunderclap. Visions of disembowelled victims at Tyburn being quartered while still living, swam before my horrified imagination.

"You've got to be joking," I protested aghast.

"You think so? Then what was that little charade in the taproom all about?"

"That?" I licked lips that had suddenly gone dry "Oh that was just — er, a spot of harmless fun."

"Harmless!" Fox-face's narrow eyes widened in a show of outraged amazement. "You call impersonating the King's Majesty harmless? Do you know what that is? — that's treason against the King's person. You know the penalty?"

Numbly, I shook my head. A cold lump seemed to be growing inside me.

"A stake at Smithfield. Picture the faggots crackling beneath

4

your feet, think of the smoke in your nostrils. Imagine the unendurable agony as the flames lick your flesh. But you can't imagine it — not without help." He nodded at the other.

There was a blur of movement and brawny fingers locked on my wrist. My hand was steered towards the candle. I fought desperately against the pressure but might as well have tried to push over London Wall. My hand was pulled above the flame...

A white-hot shaft of agony skewered my palm and a scream was ripped from my throat. Then my hand was released. I clapped it under my arm, tears of rage and pain starting from my eyes.

"Just one little candle," murmured Fox-face. "Imagine that multiplied a million times and you'll have a faint idea of what Smithfield is all about."

A red mist seemed to gather in front of my eyes. "Bastards!" I yelled. With my uninjured hand, I flung my wine in Striped-pants' face, then kicking over the table bolted for the door.

Before I had covered a yard, a vice-like hand clamped on my shoulder and I was yanked back onto my joint-stool as easily as a kitten is lifted in a cat's mouth. Unconcernedly, Striped-pants mopped his dripping face with a handkerchief.

"It bites!" said Fox-face approvingly. "It's no good trying to get away you know. Our friend here's a seasoned mercenary, veteran of a hundred campaigns — the Sack of Rome, Solway Moss, the Rough Wooing..."

"Ja — se *very* Rough Vooink," confirmed Striped-pants, dabbing his chin.

"Look — I didn't mean any harm mimicking the King," I cried. "I'm as loyal as the next man. It's ridiculous to call a silly prank treason. Anyway, who the hell gives you the right to hold me like this?"

"*We're* asking the questions," snapped Fox-face. Then he seemed to relax. "Still, I see no reason why you shouldn't know, I suppose. I hold a commission from the Kings's Secretary — Bishop Gardiner. Perhaps you think that doesn't cut much ice, because you've heard that Gardiner's under a cloud for trying to have the Queen arrested for heresy. All empty rumour; Gardiner's influence with the King has never been stronger. So if I pin a charge on you

5

laddie, it'll stick, believe me."

"I don't get it," I said. "Why me? I'm the smallest of small fry; there can't be any percentage for you in charging me with anything."

"That's as may be," replied Fox-face enigmatically "In the meantime, I'm arranging a little trip to the Marshalsea."

The Marshalsea! One of those names like Newgate or the Tower, that strike a chill to the heart. I recalled that poor old Udall had languished in the Marshalsea after his downfall from Eton.

"But — my family, they're expecting me home," I babbled. "I'm due back at Cambridge next week."

"I daresay the place will survive without you," sneered Fox-face, rising. "And now, if you'll excuse me, I have other fish to fry. You'll remain here with Martin. I'll have writing things sent in; I want you to make out a curriculum vitae. And — " he glared at me menacingly, "it had better be complete and accurate."

"Accret," repeated Martin, just in case I hadn't got the message.

The door closed behind Fox-face and I was left in the unwelcome company of the huge mercenary and my own panic-stricken thoughts.

MR STEPHENS

AFTER WRITING out my C.V. (you already know the main points), I
spent a sleepless night shivering on a straw pallet, watched over by
Martin who sat at the table playing endless games of cards against
himself and putting away prodigious quantities of wine. The pain
of my blistered palm had subsided to a dull smarting, after the
serving girl had been allowed to treat it with a soothing ointment.
The cocks had just finished crowing when a knock sounded on
the door. Martin opened it to reveal a cloaked figure.

A few murmured words passed between them then Martin
turned to me and said, "Kom." I flexed the stiffness from my
joints and accompanied them along a passageway to the front door
of the inn, where my serving-girl was waiting to let us out.

"Keep yer pecker up, Nick" she whispered, planting a kiss on
my mouth en passant, then added with a giggle, "I'll keep the
sheets warm for yer."

We hurried down the cobbled street to the riverside where a
skiff was tethered at a landing-stage. We clambered aboard, Martin
in the stern, myself in the middle and our escort in the bows.
Discarding his cloak, the boatman untied the painter and shoving
off with a sweep, manoeuvred the craft into the middle of the
stream them settled down to a long, steady stroke.

Had my circumstances been different, I would have enjoyed
that boat trip. Skeins of mist swirled up from the luminous pearly
river as the sun lifted clear of the horizon downstream. The smell
of grass and water-plants filled my nostrils; lines of duck flapped up
from the water or planed down with fountains of spray, and an
occasional heron sailed overhead. But I was in no mood to
appreciate the beauties of nature. Yesterday, I had been a carefree
student with a seduction all but in the bag; today I was a prisoner
with a charge of High Treason dangling over my head like the
sword of Damocles. The whole thing was patently trumped up,
but to what end I couldn't imagine. Martin and the boatman

ignored me when I tried talking to them; clearly they had their orders.

We pulled steadily along with the current, champion — great open fields of wheat, pasture and fallow on the Middlesex side, barren heath and woodland beyond the Surrey bank. When we reached Chiswick House, barges and wherries were beginning to displace flocks of swans, and by the time Chelsea appeared on the left, traffic was swarming on the river. The vast bulk of Westminster Abbey glided past. Then gardens and orchards, Whitehall Stairs, the great houses of nobles and statesmen — York House, Durham House, Arundel house and so forth, all running down from the Strand. We passed the Temple with its famous gardens, Whitefriars stairs leading to the thieves' warren — Alsatia, the gloomy pile of Baynard's Castle, King Henry's Palace of Bridewell, the Blackfriars' monastery already half-dismantled, and the wharves and quays piled with bales. High above a hundred others thrust the spire of St. Paul's, and ahead appeared the arches of London Bridge with its splendid houses and cluster of traitors' heads on poles above the gatehouse tower.

All around, muted by the water rose the din and bustle of the vast city. "Westward Ho!" or "Eastward Ho!" sounded faintly from the landing stairs as passengers tried to flag down boatmen. Then my stomach began to flutter like a captive bird as the boatman pulled across the stream towards the tall tower of St. Mary Overy on the Southwark side. At Paris Stairs Martin paid him off, then gripping my arm proceeded to steer me through a maze of dirty lanes, crowded with mean, furtive-looking types, stopping at last before a grim stone building — the Marshalsea.

Five days of solitary confinement in a horrible dark cell crept past, the only break in the monotony being the arrival twice a day of my gaoler with water and skilly. Once, in that period, the overflowing bucket that served as chamber pot was emptied.

I suppose all the philosophy I'd taken aboard in the Cambridge Schools should have helped me to accept my predicament with equanimity. The most practical adage I could dredge up from my memory was the third precept from the tenth book of Marcus

8

Aurelius's 'Meditations': "Whatsoever doth happen unto thee thou art either able or not able to bear. If thou beest able, be not offended but bear it according to thy natural constitution. If thou beest not able, be not offended, for it will soon make an end of thee..." So much for the benefits of a University education in helping one to Cope with Adversity.

On the sixth morning, my goaler opened my cell door to reveal two men outside. These escorted me to a waiting barge at Paris Stairs. A short way downstream, London Bridge loomed above the river; the piers of the arches, enclosed with protective timber scaffolding, made the waterways between narrow, and as swift as millraces. We shot giddily between two of these 'starlings', then my stomach began to churn — a vast complex of battlements and turrets crouching round a great square keep, loomed into view. The Tower! We rowed under an arched entrance — was this the infamous Traitor's Gate which had admitted More, Fisher, Anne Boleyn, Thomas Cromwell, Catherine Howard and a multitude of other doomed souls? I wondered.

Alighting on a slippery bank I was handed over to a goaler with a great bunch of keys at his belt. I was marched into the grim building up a staircase then along cold passages that stank of dirt and decay. Screams for help accompanied by the rattle of chains sounded from cells on either side as we passed.

"Gets yer the first time," remarked my escort. "Poor blighters yell their 'eads orf when anyone comes past. You'd think they'd get wise in time and pack it in, but they never do. You gets used ter it. This next part's a bit rough."

We hurried past pits where chained creatures, their faces no longer human, half-immersed in water fought with fiercely squeaking rats. Finally, I was halted at the entrance to a dimly-lit chamber. A stench of blood and vinegar filled my nostrils. Horror froze my brain as I noticed grisly instruments of torture hanging from a pillar.

Seated at a table with writing paraphernalia were two people, one a surpliced cleric, the other a familiar-looking figure in a dark gown — Fox-face. In the shadows at the back of the chamber I could dimly make out a second group, a man on a stool flanked by two

9

sturdy figures. Another man, soberly but richly dressed stood to one side.

"Blimey — wot've you been up to?" the gaoler whispered to me in awed tones. "Know 'oo that is in the nightgown? Just Bishop bleedin' Gardiner — the King's Secretary, that's all. You wants ter watch 'im. A proper bastard if ever there was. The bloke wot's standin' — that's Sir Anthony Knevet the lieutenant of the Tower. 'E's all right. Does 'is job an' treats a man fair — gaoler or prisoner, don't make no odds. That other one — the little creep with the crafty mug; dunno 'oo he is, 'cept that he's Arse-Licker-in-Chief to the Bishop. They'll be going to interrogate that poor bloke over there on the stool. 'You have only to answer to a few questions...' They always say that."

Fox-face murmured something to Gardiner.

The Bishop looked up, a smile on his primly good-humoured face. "Ah, the student," he said in welcoming tones. "Step forward young man. Thank you goaler. You may go."

"Take my advice," whispered the gaoler. "Tell them everything they want to know. They'll get it out of you in the end anyway. Best o' luck."

I advanced into the chamber; my knees turned weak as I spotted more torture gadgets.

"You've noticed our little toys, I see," went on Gardiner, in conversational tones. "Those are the thumbscrews —, the gauntlet —, the Scavenger's Daughter. And over there is the rack."

I felt my mouth dry out with terror as I looked at the trough-shaped contraption with windlasses at either end. The pain was unendurable, they said; even the bravest cried out for mercy on the rack.

"Don't be afraid. We only use the rack on obstinate prisoners, like our friend on the stool over there. I want you to see what happens if you're obstinate — see and take note."

Gardiner signed to the two men flanking the prisoner, rough fellows with expressionless faces — professional torturers, I guessed. The prisoner — a youngish man clad only in shirt and hose, once fine but now torn and filthy, was dragged to the rack and his ankles and wrists secured by ropes to the windlasses.

10

Gardiner went over to the prisoner. "Come, my friend," he said in reassuring tones, "you have only to answer a few questions. First — what are the names of those who met with you to discuss translating of the Scriptures?"

Beads of sweat started from the man's brow but he remained silent. Gardiner signed to the torturers to begin their work. Oars were placed into slots in the windlasses. The two men grasped the oar-handles and began to pull. Slowly the windlasses turned. The slack ropes became taut, the sagging body and limbs straightened....

A terrible shriek burst from the tortured man, then his head lolled in unconsciousness.

Vinegar was dashed in his face. The man's eyes opened, and a bubbling groan issued from his throat. The windlasses began to turn again. I gazed in horrified fascination as the victim's limbs visibly lengthened. More screams... more vinegar.... names tumbled from the victim's lips. The torturers eased the pressure on the levers and looked enquiringly at Gardiner who signed to them to continue.

Knevet stepped forward. "That's enough," he called sternly, his face creased with distaste. "Can't you see he's told you all he knows." He turned to the torturers. "Remove him."

The poor wretch's dislocated limbs were untied and he was carried from the chamber. "If you'll excuse me gentlemen." Sir Anthony bowed curtly and swept out.

"An admirable fellow Knevet," Gardiner murmured to no one in particular, "but a trifle soft-hearted." He resumed his seat at the table, then picked up a piece of paper which I recognized as my C.V. "Well, all this seems in order." He smiled at me encouragingly. "I see no reason Wainwright why you shouldn't resume your studies at Cambridge — eventually. All we require from you is a little — ah, co-operation."

I wetted dry lips. "I'll co-operate in any way I can, my Lord Bishop."

"Splendid, splendid. Then we can all forget about your little — 'indiscretion' shall we call it? at Windsor the other day." Gardiner's smiling face suddenly became serious. "Unfortunately, there's something else that has come to light." He turned to Fox-face. "Tell him. Dr. Lamb."

Lamb! That was rich, I thought.

Fox-face — Lamb, waved a slim paper-bound printed volume at me. "This is a Concordance, Wainwright," he rasped. "Do you know what that is?"

"It's — a sort of commentary on words used in Holy Scripture, I think."

"Near enough. And you know that possession of such a thing is absolutely forbidden?"

"Yes." Like everyone else, I knew all about the Six Articles (generally supposed to have been the work of 'Mr. Stephens' as Gardiner was nicknamed), and the unpleasant things that happened to those who flouted them. What was all this leading up to? I wondered. I had never been remotely tempted to get involved in religious controversy. If Henry wanted to sack the Pope and make himself Head of the Church, if he chose to dissolve the monasteries and put their loot up for grabs, if he felt like forbidding speculation about Holy Writ — that was all fine by me.

"Do you know where we found this book?"

"No." My heart gave a lurch. This elaborate charade was undoubtedly building up to some unpleasant revelation that would drive another nail into my coffin.

"We found it in a chest of books in your mother's parlour. What have you to say to that my friend?" Lamb sat back and surveyed me with a mocking leer.

A vision of my desirable stepmother going up in smoke and flames at Smithfield flashed into my mind, turning me sick. A host of futile protestations of the 'It's a rotten frame-up' variety, rose to my lips but remained unuttered. These people had me over a barrel and fighting them could only make things worse.

"What is it you want from me?" I asked helplessly.

Gardiner and Lamb exchanged smug glances.

"I'm so glad you've decided to be sensible," purred Gardiner. "Then perhaps, we can incline to leniency in these matters of treason and heresy. Just to put your mind at rest, we had your parents' house in Ely searched — to eliminate them from the

12

suspect list, we told them; we were investigating rumours of a nest of Reformers in the Fens. Your mother hasn't been charged with anything — yet; in fact she doesn't even know we've got the Concordance."

For the very good reason she never had it in the first place, you unctuous prick, I thought savagely.

"So — that, plus your peccadillo at Windsor, can stay under wraps. Unless..." Gardiner chuckled softly and let the unfinished sentence hang in the air. "Well, I think that's all for the time being," he continued in brisk tones. "Explanations tomorrow. In the meantime, the good Sir Anthony will arrange for you to have a bath, a shave and change of clothes." He eyed my unkempt figure with some distaste. "We can't have you going to Hampton Court looking like that can we?"

A GOOD ALL-ROUNDER

I GAZED out of the window over the lawns and flower-beds of the palace that had been Wolsey's before our King had cast an envious eye on it. Like beads on an abacus, craft slid back and forth marking the course of the distant river — lighters, barges, wherries plying between Staines and London.

With a sense of unreality, I looked around at the neat little bedsitter I had been allocated, and thought wryly of Marcus Aurelius. Being philosophical wasn't really all that difficult, I decided — it was just a matter of circumstances.

Came a knock on the door and a servitor asked me to accompany him. I followed the man down corridors hung with fine tapestries, and was shown into a chamber with linenfold panelling furnished as a library-cum-music-room. There were shelves of books, a pair of globes, mathematical and astronomical instruments, viols, lutes, a harpsichord — the sort of interior which German or Flemish painters depict to flatter their clients' pretensions to be Compleat Men, the 'St Jerome in his study' set piece. Although the day was far from cold, a fire of sea coal flickered in a fireplace of contemporary Gothic. A youngish man of medium height stood in the window embrasure.

"The student, Wainwright," announced the servitor and withdrew.

The man by the window turned and strode towards me with a smile; rather to my surprise he held out his hand. I had an overall impression of red and brown — brown jacket, russet gown trimmed with beaver, tanned skin with ruddy cheeks, brown beard and hair (cut short in the modern style).

"Ascham — Roger Ashcam," he announced with a trace of Yorkshire accent. "Lecturer in Greek at St. John's, Cambridge. On extended sick-leave at present — recovering from a bout of quartan fever. That's the official story. Actually I'm engaged in hush-hush work for the Goverment — more about that presently. And you're

14

Nicholas Wainwright, a Cambridge man as well. They gave me your C.V. to read; I see you've included Archery under 'Skills'."

I returned the firm handshake, liking the man immediately. He seemed to radiate warmth, straightforwardness and sturdy horse-sense — a welcome contrast to the deviousness of my recent interrogators. Ascham — the name seemed familiar. Suddenly I recalled some of my fellow-students at the Cambridge Butts eagerly discussing a forthcoming treatise on Archery written by a don.

"I'm looking forward to reading your book," I said.

Ascham's eyes lit up. "My 'Toxophilus' — it's just out. You'll have to buy a copy and I'll sign it. We must have a match some time — clouts at Finsbury, or rovers at Newington Butts. But now my friend, to business."

We drew up chairs at a table covered with a Turkey carpet and littered with papers among which I recognized a copy of my C.V.

"Before I explain what all this is about," Ascham said, looking me squarely in the face, "I think we should establish certain parameters. Your C.V. here tells me all I need to know about you. Anything else, your religion, your politics, your views on public affairs — that's your business entirely. I won't pry and I don't want to know about any of it. If Messrs. Gardiner and Lamb have some sort of hold over you — which I suspect must be the case or you'd hardly be here, you have my sympathy. But that's all. Don't try unburdening your heart — I wouldn't listen, and even if I did there's nothing I could do. Guard your tongue, do your job, mind your business and watch your back — those are the rules for survival in this game."

"Which is?"

"I'm coming to that. You've been selected for a secret assignment of vital importance. My job is to vet you and, if I think you fill the bill, to brief you about the business and arrange training and back-up facilities. The vetting's pretty well a formality. Gardiner and Lamb, whatever else they might be are shrewd judges of men; you'd not have gone this far unless they were sure they'd picked the right chap for the job. Now before I disclose anything, I must make two things absolutely clear. First — there's considerable personal risk involved. Second — if you succeed, the slate will be

15

wiped clean concerning any trouble you may be in, in addition to which you'll be handsomely rewarded."

"That's easy to say," I broke in bitterly. "From my experience of Gardiner and Lamb, I wouldn't trust either of them round the corner."

"My own sentiments exactly — you didn't hear that, by the way. Actually, to be fair to Gardiner he did recommend my book to the King, who was gracious enough to grant me a pension as a result. Gardiner may have chosen you but he won't be your boss. You'll be working for someone higher."

Wriothesley the Chancellor? I wondered. No — the Secretary outranked the Great Seal. Secretary Paget — that faceless wonder? But Gardiner was senior Secretary. There *was* no one higher. Then realization dawned on me...

"You mean — the King!"

Ascham nodded gravely, an expression of what I can only term resolute devotion transforming his features. In a flash of intuition, I knew that here was a 'King's Man' — one of those in whom Henry's famous personal magnetism had inspired selfless loyalty, a category of servant a world removed from time-serving opportunists like 'Mr. Stephens' and other Court toadies who curried Henry's favour for their own advancement. (Perhaps I was being unfair to Gardiner and letting my judgement be clouded by personal experience; some have described him as disinterestedly efficient.) I assumed that Ascham couldn't know about my little impersonation at Windsor.

"Well — do you agree to take the job?" asked Ascham, looking at me intently. "I can't tell you what it is I'm afraid, unless I know that you'll accept it. Security, you understand."

"Do I have a choice?"

Ascham shrugged. "Knowing our friendly neighbourhood Bishop of Winchester's little ways, I should say probably not." He smiled wryly. "After all, what can you expect from a Trinity Hall man? But if you agree, you can forget about Gardiner. He then becomes just a wooden stamp as far as you're concerned. You'll be working through me and I'll be reporting directly to His Majesty. You'll be serving the King not Gardiner, and His Grace is generous to those who serve him well. By the way, your — 'sabbatical' shall we call it? from Cambridge has been made all official. No problem, as Gardiner's chancellor of the University. Also a letter will be sent to your parents explaining that you have been seconded for an ambassadorial mission — or some such flannel."

I took a deep breath and heard myself say, "Very well — I accept."

"Good man. This calls for a drink." Ascham rose and went to a cupboard. "Have a goblet of sack. Shipped direct from the Jerez bodegas. There may be a war on but we can still get the stuff out from Spain."

"What I can't understand," I said, rolling the sack on my tongue and savouring its full-bodied flavour, "is — why me? I'm just an ordinary undergraduate from an ordinary family. No wealth, no important connections, no great talent for anything in particular. I just don't get it."

"Before I tell you what the job is, let me explain the sort of candidate we were looking for. Basically, we weren't trying to find any kind of paragon or heavyweight. What we were after was an intelligent all-rounder with the ability to think on his feet and adapt quickly to varying situations. He should be well-informed, be able to use his initiative, and mix freely with all ranks of society. He must also be fit and strong. I'd say you filled the bill pretty neatly." Ascham sipped sack and looked at me appraisingly.

He reached forward and picked up my C.V. "'Education — Kings' Ely and Cambridge'," he paraphrased. "Which means, you've rubbed shoulders with all types from butcher's sons to earls. You've learned to hold your own — academically and socially, or you wouldn't have stayed the course at Cambridge, as I know from my own experience. 'Track Record — business trips undertaken occasionally on behalf of your father, to chandlers, merchants and dealers in Peterborough, Norwich, Thetford and Kings's Lynn, besides numerous negotiations with local farmers. One extended trip to Antwerp.' Well, it goes without saying that you must have acquired something in the way of diplomatic skills and business acumen. 'Languages — French, Latin, a little Low Dutch and Spanish.' You'd have picked those last two up in the Low

17

Countries I suppose. 'Skills and Accomplishments — shooting at the Butts, best score five whites and eight blacks over three ends at eleven score yards:' Not bad; the 1542 Act stipulates that range for twenty-four years and over, and you're what — twenty-two, twenty-three? 'Music, able to sight read and sing a tenor part, also some skill on the guitar and a little on the lute: Book-keeping.' Your musical ability can be useful socially, as the entrée to pub or manor-house, something that may come in handy in the sort of work you'll be doing."

Ascham recharged our goblets, then continued to read: "'Referees — Robert Steward alias Wells M.A. Cantab., Dean of Ely Cathedral formerly Prior of Ely Monastery, and a governor of the Kings' School; address, the Deanery, Ely, Cambs: John Caius M.A. Cantab, Fellow of Gonville Hall, M.D. Padua; publications — 'De Medendi Methodo', Basle, 1544 'Galen', Basle 1544 (dedicated to King Henry VIII), also 'Of English Dogs',1536 (to have formed part of Gesner's 'Natural History' but publication postponed owing to death of editor); address, c/o Barber-Surgeons' Hall, London.'"

Ascham looked up from the C.V. "There's a P.S. Gardiner has added his own comments, based on the above and Lamb's assessment of you. You may as well hear them. 'The subject appears to be intelligent and enterprising. While displaying a regrettable proclivity towards 'wine, women and song', in other respects he seems admirably suited for the task. When sufficiently provoked, reacts with commendable spirit but has the good sense not to remain obdurate when to do so would clearly be non-productive. He is an excellent mimic, which is of course vital to the role he will be called upon to play.'"

Ascham glanced at me keenly. "You'll have to watch the 'wine and women' bit. In the sort of work you'll be doing, it may be important to be able to hold your liquor, also a way with the ladies could be advantageous. But *you* have to be in control — otherwise you'd be of no use to us, in fact you'd be a dangerous liability." He dropped the C.V. on the table. "Provided you never forget that, I'd say you were just the man we're — "

Without warning, the door flew open. Brandishing a sword, a

18

huge negro burst into the room and rushed straight at Ascham, who stood stock-still, as though stunned by shock.

For a moment, I too was paralyzed by this apparition. Then, acting instinctively I whipped the Turkey carpet from the table and flung it in the face of the would-be assassin, yelling at Ascham to run for the door. Like the net of a Roman retiarius, the carpet enfolded the black's head; while he tore at it with his free hand I thrust a foot between his legs and kicked up with all my strength. The man overbalanced, cannoned against the table and crashed into the wall with a crunch of wood and pinging of stings from a lute that was propped there.

"Quick man — don't just stand there!" I yelled at Ascham who, incredibly, hadn't moved.

But Ascham continued to stand there, a chuckle escaping from his lips, while the negro grinning broadly, untangled himself from the carpet and the debris of the shattered lute. It had all happened so quickly that papers were still fluttering down to the floor.

Anger fought with astonishment inside me. Then the humour of the situation got to me and I too began to chuckle. Soon the three of us were laughing uncontrollably, the tears rolling down our faces.

"Sorry about that," apologized Ascham, when his fellow-conspirator had departed. "But I had to be sure about you. I'm glad to say you passed the test with flying colours."

"And just suppose I hadn't?" I decided to put the boot in a little. I'd earned the right if anyone had. "Then you'd have had an embarrassing liability on your hands, wouldn't you? How would you have resolved that one, I wonder? A stiletto between the ribs one dark night? That would be Lamb's way, I'd imagine. Or perhaps indefinite detention pending His Majesty's pleasure. You could even have let me go I suppose, though I'm not sure Gardiner would have approved. On the whole I'm glad the question's an academic one. Just tell me what, as a Good All-Rounder, I'm actually going to do."

"Festina lente — all in good time my friend. First, a lesson in History, Geography and Current Affairs — Cosmography in other words."

19

THE COURT OF GREEN GINGER

"FORGIVE ME if it turns out that I'm teaching granny to suck eggs," said Ascham, conducting me to a large mounted globe, after we had replaced the carpet and papers. "But it's essential you have a clear grasp of the background situation before I brief you about specifics. First — you've got to understand the significance of the changes that have taken place in the last two generations. Today's world of 1545 would, in several respects, be unrecognizable to our grandfathers. Take the political dimension." He spun the globe and placed a forefinger in the Black Sea then proceeded to circumscribe Europe and the Near East. "In the fifteenth Century we had a tangle of piddling jurisdictions, still semi-feudal in some respects."

"I take your point," I said, looking at the neat boundary lines on the globe. "France, Spain, Sweden, The Holy Roman Empire, Russia, Turkey and so on — national consolidation you could call it, I suppose."

"Precisely. And that process has been paralleled by staggering technological progress accompanied by a tremendous acceleration in the imparting of information. The only reason the Reformation got going in our own time rather than with Wycliffe or Huss, is that Luther's little bombshell at Wittenberg only took a fortnight to spread throughout Germany. Thanks to the modern printing press, which is a great advance on Gutenberg's prototype. A century ago, we'd only the haziest notion of what the world outside Europe was like. Now, thanks to the discoveries of the Portuguese and others, allied to a revolution in shipbuilding, we know the size and shape of the continents and are beginning to penetrate their interiors. The world's been circumnavigated. European warships are no longer mere platforms for carrying soldiers, their tactics limited to grappling and boarding. They're mobile gun batteries, manoeuverable in any direction, whatever way the wind's blowing, and capable of pounding an enemy at ranges up to a mile. You've only to think of the King's flagship the *Mary Rose*.

"In the past, the armed knight who formed the spearhead of most armies was pretty well self-sufficient, needing only food and minor running repairs to his gear. Now he's been swept from the battlefield — heavy artillery plus infantry armed with pikes, bows and guns have seen to that. Modern gunpowder, field artillery and hand-guns are vastly more efficient and reliable than the uncorned powder, crude bombards and hand cannon of our grandfathers' time, and — although I hate to admit it, threaten to take over from the good old longbow. Of course all this needs a complex infrastructure to sustain it — factories, a skilled work force, raw materials, mining and metallurgical entrepreneurs, boffins, transport facilities, capitalists and bankers. And the modern nation-states that have grown up in our own time have been developing just such infastructures."

"The way you put it makes it sound as though Europe's a collection of powder-magazines just waiting for someone to drop a match!"

"Not a bad metaphor. The present situation *is* a horribly dangerous one — more so than most of those in power realize. In the past, given the fairly primitive resources available, wars tended to be small-scale affairs, their effects limited to particular localities. Now, given what can fairly be described as an Arms Race, and the build up of national strike forces of awesome potential, we are only one step away from Armageddon. The only way to contain the risk of a European blood bath, is for a Balance of Power to be maintained. A difficult feat when you think of what the weights on the pans are. In one pan you've got Charles V. That means, in addition to the clout which the title of Holy Roman Emperor carries, the Hapsburg lands in Austria and Germany, the Low Countries, the buffer strip between France and Germany, Spain and, wait for it — Mexico and Peru with their vast wealth in bullion to sustain Charles's power-bloc. Sitting in the same pan is our King Henry, and England can make quite a difference to the tilt of the scales; since '37 when Aske's Pilgrimage of Grace was squashed, she's become a strong, united state."

"And in the other pan — just poor old Francis I of France," I

21

observed. "Surely he doesn't balance Charles and Henry together?"

"I agree that on paper France looks heavily outweighed. But remember that France is a large, populous, wealthy, unified country with an efficient system of centralized government, and, thanks largely to Joan of Arc over a hundred years ago, a strong sense of national identity. By comparison, Charles's dominions are scattered and lack any natural bonding — positively centrifugal in fact. Anyway, France doesn't stand alone. She has a good friend in Scotland who's always ready to stab England in the back if we move our armies across the channel. Also, since 1536, France has been allied with Turkey."

"Turkey! But that's a whole new ball game. A Christian Kingdom joining with a Muslim Empire — That doesn't seem to be quite playing the game somehow."

"Don't be naive, my friend — this is this sixteenth century; all's fair in love and war, needs must when the devil drives and so forth. Naturally Charles makes what capital he can out of it, holds his hands up in horror and accuses Francis of betraying Christendom — Europe if you like; 'Let's keep things in our own camp, chaps.' Which is just so much pious cant of course; Christendom's a dead duck in these Reforming times. Still, France's mésalliance with Suleiman the Magnificent does introduce a dangerous new dimension into modern power politics. The consolidation of the Turkish Ottoman Empire into a totalitarian state with a crack Janissary army, and its penetration into Europe since 1453, now threaten Europe's very existence. It's less than two years since Hungary was finally taken over by the Turks. Since the Crusades fizzled out centuries ago, do you know which is the only force permanently mobilized against the Turks? The Knights of Malta, formerly of Rhodes. As a serious deterrent it's a sick joke."

"So not only is Europe in danger of destroying itself with its dangerous new toys, it could also be overwhelmed from the East?"

"You've got it in one. If Turkey were the only threat, that would be bad enough. But — look here." Ascham's finger touched a point on the globe to the north of the Ottoman Empire.

"Russia?" I asked, vaguely puzzled. The name conjured up a picture of a primitive, semi-barbaric country on the fringe of

Europe, Christian to be sure, but of a type of Christianity so disparate from the Western form, as to make the divergences between the Roman and Reformed Churches seem positively ecumenical.

"Russia," confirmed Ascham. "Up till now, no one's bothered to take Russia seriously. Until just before the end of our own Wars of the Roses, it was a mere province of the Tatar Khan of the Golden Horde. Then, in 1480, Ivan III renounced his allegiance and declared himself Tsar. Russia may be backward but she's a trading country and was able to defend Moscow's Kremlin with cannon and muskets obtained from the West — more than a match for the Tatar horse-archers. In fact, the tide has now turned the other way. Using the new technology, Ivan IV — Ivan the Terrible as he's known, is pushing Russia's frontiers across the Tatar lands deep into Central Asia. He's all set to take Kagan and Astrakhan. If he does, he'll have a line of river communications by way of the Caspian all the way to Persia."

"But if Russia's preoccupied with Eastern expansion, where's the threat to Europe?" I objected.

"I'm coming to that. You see, Sweden and Poland are nibbling at Russia's western borders, so Ivan has a ready-made 'casus belli'. Also, he wants a window on the Baltic, to match the one he's about to gain on the Caspian. Ivan's successfully transforming Russia into a state that's even more totalitarian than the Ottoman Empire. He's decimating the old noble class — the boyars, who might challenge his authority, and replacing them with a secret bureaucracy of 'service nobility' as they're called, who'll do exactly as they're told.

"However, if it came to a shooting war between Russia on the one hand, and Sweden plus Poland on the other, it's questionable if Russia could do much more than hold her own. The technology and wealth gap's just too wide at present. But if Russia ever manages to close that gap… " Ascham let the sentence trail away, and looked at me bleakly. "Well, she could prove to be a threat to Western civilization even more menacing than the Turks.

"But that's to speculate about the future. To turn to more immediate matters — you know that our campaign in Scotland has more or less ground to a halt?"

I nodded. Next to the King's capture of Boulogne, the news had been of little else than the Scottish Front.

"Tell me what you know," asked Ascham quietly. I sensed that he wished to check not only my knowledge, but my understanding of the political situation. I was reasonably well-informed. More and more, the custom of noblemen educating their sons by sending them to live at other noblemen's houses, was being replaced by sending them to University. Consequently, there was at Cambridge an ever-growing number of sons of great families, who tended to regard affairs of state almost as their personal preserve, so that the Cambridge air was always thick with Court gossip and news of great doings. I've heard it said that provided you could sort the wheat from the chaff, you could be as well-informed at Cambridge as a King's minister in Westminster.

"Well, it all started after Solway Moss, two and a half years ago," I said, choosing my words carefully. "Wharton smashed a vastly superior Scots army at that battle. As a result, James V of Scotland died of a broken heart, they say, leaving the newborn infant Mary as Queen." I glanced at Ascham to see how I was doing but his face gave away nothing. Then I remembered — Ascham; wasn't that the name of an erstwhile tutor of Prince Edward and Princess Elizabeth? This must surely be the same man. Certainly, in his air of attention and quiet authority there was something of the pedagogue.

"With the Kings of Scots dead, the Scots leaders quarreling and their army shattered, we could probably have invaded successfully," I pressed on self-consciously, feeling like a schoolboy reciting a lesson. "But our King Henry thought of a better plan. If he could arrange for his five year old son Edward to marry the baby Scots Queen, then the two kingdoms would eventually come under one ruler. Result — a United Kingdom and the end of the eternal Scottish Problem. Negotiations were started and at first seemed to be going well."

"Full marks so far," murmured Ascham. "What went wrong with the scheme?"

"I'm not absolutely clear about the details but I think the Scots

24

began to feel they were being pressurized — always a mistake where they're concerned. Somehow, negotiations broke down, whereupon our King lost patience with the Scots and decided to use force to make them accept his policy. Hertford sacked and burned Leith and Edinburgh while Wharton and Eure, the wardens, laid waste the Border, backed up, I believe, by renegade Scots. Mission accomplished, Hertford returned home, but Eure, with the help of foreign mercenaries, remained to polish off Southern Scotland. Those mercenaries — a pretty wild bunch, I'm told."

"That's putting it mildly," murmured Ascham. "The scum of Europe — Germans, Italians, French, Spanish. Terrible people. I can't help feeling a sneaking sympathy for the Scots. They may be a 'beastly and unreasonable people' to quote young Ralph Sadleyr, one of the unfortunates who was given the job of trying to implement the marriage proposals, but I sometimes think that wielding the big stick can be counter-productive as regards our Northern neighbours. Sorry — you were saying?"

"Well, the Earl of Angus, helped by the Earl of Arran, moved south in February of this year to sort out the renegade Borderers who were helping Eure. Eure hurried to defend his allies but was somehow outmanoeuvred at Ancrum Moor near Jedburgh. His army was badly beaten and Eure himself was killed. As a result, it's now rumoured that the French are prepared to send troops to help Scotland. That's about all I can tell you, I'm afraid."

"Don't be," said Ascham approvingly. "You've summarised the sequence of events really rather neatly." Then his voice became grave. "Ancrum Moor should never have happened. Eure outnumbered Angus's men by ten to one. All right — so they were ambushed, and had to fight with the sun in their faces. As an explanation of such an annihilating defeat, that just doesn't hold water. Granted, the 'assured Scots' on Eure's side deserted when they saw the tide turning against them. But that's the whole point — the tide *shouldn't* have turned. Eure's huge numerical superiority should have easily cancelled out a relatively minor tactical disadvantage."

"Perhaps Eure's lot were caught napping?" I suggested.

"Absolutely not. They were in full service marching order and trying to make contact with the enemy. When I said that they were ambushed, all that that amounted to was that Angus managed to conceal the bulk of his piddling little army until Eure was right up to them."

"But what other explanation is there?" I asked, experiencing a prickle of expectation. I had a feeling that we were approaching the nub of the whole business.

"What I'm about to tell you is in the strictest confidence," said Ascham. "Not a word to be breathed outside this room. You understand?" ·

"Understood."

"Very well. It's my belief that at Ancrum Moor, the Scots employed for the first time, a secret weapon of devastating power and effectiveness."

"Evidence?"

"That's the problem — what there is is so nebulous and fragmentary as to seem virtually non-existent. Yet I'm convinced there's a pattern — a tenuous one admittedly, that lends support to my theory."

"Like what?"

"Reliable reports from scouts some days prior to the battle, say that Angus's army were armed mainly with lances. We know that a large part of Eure's force had firearms, and — apart from the regrettable fact that as usual, there weren't enough longbowmen, Eure's soldiers were in general better armed and equipped than Angus's. Yet what was the outcome? Nearly a thousand of Eure's men killed and over a thousand taken prisoner. Don't tell me that begins to make any sense — not unless there's a factor that hasn't been taken into account, somewhere."

"And you think such a factor exists?"

"Yes. My belief rests on statements made by some of the survivors. The majority of course are still in Scots prisons waiting to be ransomed so we won't get any corroboration for some time. This is what some of those escapees spoke of — rapid and continuous fire from a few points on the enemy front, which had devastating results. Here are some of their actual words as near as I can remember: 'As if a hundred backbutters standing in the same

26

place were firing one after the other...' and, 'A withering blast of sustained fire before which our men melted like snow off a dyke...' and, 'Bullets from an invisible source cut down our men in windrows...' and so on. The striking thing is the consistency of the various accounts."

"You said that a lot of Eure's — 'assured Scots' I think you called them, went over to Angus," I pointed out. "Couldn't they have accounted for the increased firepower?"

"Not on the scale or in the manner which the evidence would seem to point to. Besides, the Scottish Borderers don't go in for guns much, preferring lances and things called 'Jedart staves' — a sort of poleaxe."

"What about the dead? Wouldn't their wounds give some clue as to the sort of weapon that had killed them?"

"The dead seem to have been buried quickly, on the spot. And Angus was hardly going to allow English survivors to carry out post-mortems."

"What are you suggesting actually happened?" I asked. A premonition that I was about to hear something terrible, seemed to touch my spine with a cold finger.

Ascham looked at me levelly. "I believe that the Scots were using some sort of gun capable of firing many bullets in succession without having to be reloaded."

"But that's imposible!"

"Is it? I admit that until Ancrum Moor I'd have said the same. But I've chewed the matter over in my mind ad nauseam, and I can't come up with any other explanation. Remove the impossible and whatever you're left with, however improbable, must be the truth, as some Greek philosopher says. Of course we do know of guns that can fire more than one shot; a pistol with revolving barrels has been developed in Italy and a chap in Nuremburg has produced one with a fixed barrel and revolving cylinder holding several charges. Even a century ago the Hussite wagenbergs mounted guns capable of multiple fire — several gunbarrels fixed together and touched off in turn or all together. But these revolvers and 'organs' are only volley-guns capable of producing short bursts of fire. At Ancrum Moor, I'm convinced that Eure's troops were exposed to sustained

27

multiple-fire — a very different proposition."

"All right — let's allow for the sake of argument, that the Scots have a gun capable of producing the effect you've described. How would it work?"

"Lacking anything in the way of hard evidence, I can only speculate. But there are two points that we can be pretty sure of, I think. For sustained multiple-fire to be possible, a breech-loading system would be obligatory. Nothing new in that of course. The King's Grace possesses several breech-loading carbines, for example. Then, you would have to have your powder and shot pre-packed in cartridge cases — again, by no means a novel idea. What has so far frustrated the development of a gun capable of rapid-fire is the impossibility of securing a gas-tight seal at the breech, also the devising of a lock, capable of detonating the cartridge in a more efficient and rapid manner than the present system of an external snap-lock igniting the charge through a touch-hole."

"And you think the Scots have discovered a solution to these problems?"

Ascham looked at me bleakly and shrugged. "I wish there were a different conclusion I could arrive at."

"But why did nobody actually see what was producing this — 'stream of bullets' or whatever you called it?"

"There are several possible reasons, I think. The sun was setting in the faces of Eure's men, remember. Also the smoke of their own gunfire was blown back in their faces, according to reports. So-called 'assured Scots' were deserting right and left. A chaotic situation. The fire may have issued from behind prepared positions or been from long range — a good modern handgun can shoot 600 yards."

Silence settled between us, while the implication of what Ascham had been saying blossomed in my mind like some monstrous flower.

"That means — if you're right, and assuming the Scots have enough of these things, that we'll lose the war in Scotland. And if the French get them from their Scottish allies ..."

"... the Balance of Power will be destroyed," Ascham finished the sentence for me, in grim tones. "The stability of Europe will collapse like a house of cards, and a holocaust of destruction be let loose. Either that or an Arms Race which could result in European civilization destroying itself."

"Or one nation becoming a super-power and swallowing up the rest?" I suggested. "God — what if the Turks or the Russians were to get hold of this thing? But perhaps we're over-playing Devil's Advocate. Do you really think the results would be as catastrophic as you suggest?"

"They would be more so, in all likelihood. But I think we would be advised to drop the conditional for the future tense. I believe we are talking not about what would happen, if — , but what *will* happen, when — . Unless... "

"Unless this secret weapon is discovered and destroyed," I said. Then a chilling realization of my likely role crept over me.

"Exactly. A search and destroy mission. It should be fairly clear from my earlier resumé of the qualities needed for the job, why you've been chosen. We want you to go into Scotland — under a cover role of course, find out where the secret weapon is being manufactured then destroy it, and the plant. I suspect that at Ancrum Moor they were testing a prototype weapon and that they won't have gone into full production yet."

"I see — just like that," I sneered bitterly. The appalling risk of the job began to register; I experienced a wave of terror and resentment in about equal proportions. "I suppose you think it's a simple matter to march into a hostile war-zone, sniff out the whereabouts of this infernal machine, which is bound to be more securely guarded than St. Edward's Regalia, and knock it out. And where on earth does one start looking?"

"I can't blame you for feeling the way you do," said Ascham gently. "But it's not quite such a hopeless proposition as you seem to imagine. I think we can safely say that the weapon's not imported — any country capable of manufacturing it would surely keep it for its own defence or for purposes of aggression. Assuming that it's being produced in Scotland, we can narrow down the possible sites.

"Clearly the weapon must be mainly constructed of metal — bronze or steel in all probability. Skilled artisans are essential to make and assemble it. Charcoal and coal will be required for

29

smelting and forging — if steel is a component, iron-ore will be a raw material. These raw materials are bulky and heavy, therefore difficult to transport long distances, to say nothing of cost — impossibly difficult in a combat zone. The craftsmen, whether foreign or Scots, will be members of guilds of hammermen, i.e. metalworkers; these corporations are only to be found in the burghs. So what we're looking for is a large to fair-sized burgh, either with port facilities for importing bar-iron or raw materials, or with the raw materials fairly close at hand. With Scotland's foreign trade disrupted by the war, I'd plump for the latter alternative. So where does that leave us?"

"You tell me," I said drily.

Ascham rummaged among the papers on the table and produced a printed map of Scotland.

"Beautiful, isn't it?" he enthused. "George Lyly. From a copperplate for his Atlas of Britain. It's gone to the printers but I persuaded him to let me have a spare galley-proof. It's really accurate and up-to-date — based on a recent survey by Alexander Lindsay." He spread the map out and pointed with his forefinger. "As you see, the burghs are mainly to be found down the East coast, in the Central Lowlands and a few in the valleys of the Southern Uplands. Coal and iron-ore deposits are fairly common in the Central Lowlands, especially in the western parts. I think therefore we can safely forget about the Highlands. The Borders and South-East Scotland are a war-zone, which probably puts them out of the running. Otherwise, Edinburgh would be the ideal site. But over here — " his forefinger traced an ellipse around the Clyde valley, "you've got burghs like Glasgow, Ayr and Lanark — with raw materials at hand, well out of the fighting area, and with the necessary infrastructure. If I were a betting man — which I regret to say I am, I would put my money on that being your general area of search."

We looked at each other over the map for long seconds.

"Look," I said at length, "I'm flattered by your high opinion of my qualifications. But I still don't see why I was singled out. There must be any number of people more suitable than myself. Besides, I've never been to Scotland, and I know virtually nothing about the place. Anyway, my accent would be a dead give-away."

"Don't play yourself down, my friend. Good men aren't so thick on the ground as you seem to think. And Lamb doesn't usually make mistakes. Also you're forgetting that one of the reasons why Lamb chose you was your gift of mimicry. I've no doubt that given a bit of practice, you could pass yourself off as a Scot. That'll be part of your training. We'll supply a tame Scot who'll give you elocution lessons."

They seemed to have thought of everything. "Who's 'we?'" I asked.

"Strictly, that's something as an agent, you don't 'need to know'. But — unlike some others that I could name, I maintain that an informed spy, provided his discretion is to be trusted, can be more useful than a blinkered one.

"Well, apart from myself, who first guessed at the probable truth of what happened at Ancrum Moor and convinced the others, there's just Gardiner, Secretary Paget, Lamb, and the King, Nobody else. We've constituted ourselves into 'The Court of Green Ginger'."

"The Court of *what*?"

"Don't laugh. There's a place in Hull called the Land of Green Ginger — presumably the stuff's imported there; a convenient half-way house between Westminster and the Northern Front. I've a merchant friend whose house is in the Land of Green Ginger. From time to time, some of us — usually just me, rendezvous there with Marcher Wardens or their emissaries, to hear Intelligence reports on the situation in the war-zone and in Scotland generally.

"As a Yorkshireman with contracts throughout the North, I've been appointed Secretary. The organization's simple and streamlined — none of the tedious rigmarole you get with normal government machinery. I'm in charge of overall planning and correspondence, and prepare the necessary writs and warrants; Gardiner franks them with the Royal Sign Manual stamp that the King has had made for him — and that's it. We're really a State Department in miniature, a secret one."

"How exactly do I go about getting into Scotland?"

"We thought your best cover would be an amateur physician —

a travelling quacksalver, in other words. We'll supply all the gear and medicines, naturally, and you'll be given proper instruction in the basics of your craft. All part of the training course. As a quacksalver, you can go anywhere — from castle to cottage, without exciting suspicion, and generally gain entrée to places that would otherwise be barred to you. As for getting over the frontier — that's all being taken care of. You'll be given details nearer the time."

Ascham paused and looked at me, a pucker of concern between his eyebrows. "You'll appreciate that we're up against a deadline. We have to locate and eliminate this menace with the minimum possible delay. So your training will be something of a crash course, I'm afraid. Well, that's all I can tell you. Any questions?"

There were only about a hundred I felt like asking, but my reply was in the negative.

PASTIME WITH GOOD COMPANY

THE NEXT three weeks passed in a blur of gruelling activity. The day following my interview with Ascham, my combat training began in the grounds of the Palace — virtually deserted except for gardeners and cleaners, as the Court was elsewhere.

I was under the tutelage of Martin, the huge mercenary whose acquaintance I had first made at Windsor. As a young Lanzknecht, he had seen service at Pavia, since when his life had been a succession of sieges, pitched battles, forced marches, sorties and raids. (All this I had from Ascham, for Martin divulged nothing to me about his life.) There seemed to be no aspect of modern infantry warfare with which he was not familiar (including pillage and rapine, I had no doubt) and, with the single exception of the longbow, he was an expert with all the weapons of the footsoldier — hackbut, caliver, the heavier musket, pistol, crossbow, bill, lance, spear, rapier, dagger and sword. (His own sword was a monstrously long two-handed affair, which he carried slung behind his back.)

Under Martin's brutally efficient guidance, I learned to acquit myself passably with dagger, sword and carbine. (This last was a wheel-lock from the King's own armoury, the charge contained in an iron cartridge case loading at the breech.) I also learned, painfully, about Unarmed Combat — how to creep up on someone undetected, how to disable an armed man using feet and hands as weapons, the killing-points where a blow of the fist or edge of the palm would bring instant death, and many more interesting little tricks.

I was forced to trot for miles in full service marching order — steel helmet, padded body-armour, gun, ammunition pouches, short sword, provisions pack, until I dropped, whereupon Martin would stolidly proceed to kick me in the more tender parts of my anatomy until I tottered to my feet.

At the end of a week, I felt as if my body were one vast aching bruise. I was so slogged-out each night that I could only collapse on my bed, to plunge instantly into dreamless sleep till summoned by Martin for another day of killing exertion. By the end of the second week, my stiffness was easing and I was beginning to feel sufficiently human to pass the odd evening with Ascham; I would accompany his excellent lute-playing on a vihuela, the nearest instrument I could find to a guitar, or we would play chess or a hand of cards, or just talk.

I felt that our relationship was becoming less that of spymaster and spy, than of friends. Everyone who was rising in the world seemed to have taken a leaf from Machiavelli's 'Prince', and to be doing so by standing on the necks of others. Ascham was a pleasant exception to this trend. Open, straightforward, a scholar who wore his learning lightly, a skilled musician and an exquisite penman in the new Italic style, a great archer, a pioneer in the field of education (he was unique among pedagogues in opposing corporal punishment), here was a man one could like and admire, to serve whom was a privilege rather than a burdensome duty.

But most of what little spare time I had, was spent in turning myself into a Scot. My tutor was a slim, soft-spoken, strikingly handsome youth, one Walter Ker — the scion of some pretty tribe with illusions of nobility, from the wrong side of the Border. He had been captured in some skirmish and was being held pending ransom. He had been promised that this would be waived and he would be set free unconditionally, if he succeeded in turning me into a passable Scot. Despite his gentle voice, and good looks which a pretty woman might have envied, there was nothing effeminate about Ker. His manner was forthright, sometimes to the extent of bluntness, and his accounts of raids, feuding, blackmail and bloody reprisals — the small change of life on the Border, I gathered, had the ring of personal experience. (Ascham had half-hinted with an accompanying wink, that the 'capture' might have been stage-managed. "Ker's one of your few 'assured Scots' who *can* be trusted," he went on to affirm. "And that's all I'm saying," he concluded mysteriously.)

Thanks to my talent for mimicry and my smattering of Low Dutch, I made rapid progress under Ker's tuition. The Dutch and Scots languages share the same guttural 'ch' sound, and I was able to cope straight away with 'loch', 'nicht', 'fecht' and so on. In a few days I had mastered the language and mannerisms to the extent of drawing from Ker a laconic, "Ye're comin oan" — praise indeed from a Border Scot. I was coached in the deportment and customs of the Frontier — a smoothly lying tongue, a high opinion of oneself, a cavalier disregard for property, especially other people's, and an entrenched belief in the survival of the fittest.

From maps traced with a stick in flower beds, I learned the courses of the rivers and the lie of the valleys of the Borderland, till I think I could have made my way from Kelso to Langholm, or Hawick to the Merse without any problem. True, I would only be passing through the Borders en route to the West Central belt, but as my persona was that of a Border Scot, it was essential to be au fait with the background details.

But the most important — and difficult, thing of all which I had to acquire was 'atmosphere'. (It was Ascham who insisted on this.) It wasn't enough just to mimic the speech of a Scots itinerant and swot up topographical details. You had to think yourself into the part until you *were* it.

From Ker I learned too something of the appalling destruction and brutality being inflicted on Southern Scotland — mainly by the foreign mercenaries it is true, but with the full knowledge and consent of the English commanders, For the first time, I found myself querying the rightness of our policy towards the Scots; that the end — the unification of the two kingdoms, was correct surely no right-thinking person could deny; but could it justify such bloodthirsty means? No doubt Sadleyr was accurate in describing the Scots as 'beastly and unreasonable'. Still... What was it Marcus Aurelius had said? 'Him that offends, teach with love and meekness to show him his error. But if thou canst not, then blame thyself.' (Somehow, I didn't see that advice going down too well with our King!)

On what was to prove my last day of training (I didn't know it then), Martin told me to be at the tennis-court at ten o'clock that night.

I arrived before the appointed time and waited in the darkness beside the enclosing wall. Martin arrived, unlocked the door and we entered.

"Presently, a French prisoner vill choin you inside se tennis court. You vill stay here until vun of you is no longer alive."

Something hard was pressed in my hand, the door shut behind me and the lock clicked. I felt the object into my hand — a stiletto! I felt sick and horrified. My palms began to sweat and I could feel my heart pounding in my chest. Would I actually be able to stick this thing into another man?

I crouched a few feet from the enclosed door. Pitch-dark it might be, but the lock as it opened must give some sound, enough to let me know when my opponent was entering the court. I would wait till he was inside, then...

Time crawled past. My nerves felt taut as wound-up lute strings. I could feel sweat starting from my armpits and dribbling between my shoulder blades.

A faint scuffling sound *above* me! I looked up, caught a momentary glimpse of a shadowy silhouette on the penthouse roof. Then the man crashed into me and I was lying flat on my back, the wind knocked out of me and the dagger jerked from my hand with the impact. Hands closed round my throat. A roaring filled my head and I felt my senses begin to swim. Desperately, my hand scrabbled on the floor, touched something hard, closed on the handle of the dagger. With all my failing strength I drove it into the shape above me, felt the blade go in to the hilt, a warm spurt of blood on my hand. The pressure on my throat eased; a cry of surprise and pain broke from my assailant then suddenly ended in a choking gurgle. The man rolled clear of my body and I rose groggily onto my knees, my wheezing lungs sucking in air like bellows.

Gradually, my breathing returned to normal. I located my attacker's pulse; he was dead. Only then did it come to me that he hadn't been armed. I leaned against the penthouse rails and was violently sick.

Next morning, in a fury, I sought out Ascham. "You can keep your mission," I shouted. "Gardiner and Lamb may have me by the short hairs, but I won't be treated like an early Christian in the arena. I could have been killed last night. As it was, I had to murder

36

a defenceless man in cold blood." I proceeded to give him the details.

"God Nicholas — I knew nothing about this, I swear." Ascham's horrified disgust seemed genuine. "Must have been Lamb — just his style; his way of checking that you had enough 'bottle' for the task ahead, I suppose. Well, this time he's gone too far. He'll be cut down to size — that I promise you."

Ascham's tone changed and a note of excitement crept into his voice as he pulled a document from inside his jacket; "I've just received this. The King wishes to speak to you personally. We'll take a barge down to Whitehall Palace with the tide."

My rage, mollified anyway to some extent by Ascham's reaction evaporated at this extraordinary news.

We got off at Whitehall Stairs. This, being a general landing stage allowed public right of way through the Palace. Formerly York Place, this was a miniature city of red-brick buildings, gardens, galleries, yards, courts and gatehouses, that rambled from Scotland Yard to St. James's Palace, with the huge Cockpit Gate straddling the highway from Charing Cross to Westminister.

Ascham seemed to know his way about this amazing warren. I followed him up the Stairs then through passages and courtyards filled with jostling throngs, to a postern where he knocked. A chamberlain admitted us and on being shown Ascham's document, conducted us along corridors painted in grotesque patterns of intertwining leaves and shoots. We passed a huge wall-painting depicting King Henry as a towering god-like figure, exuding a terrible authority. Reaching a hallway, we were asked to wait.

I was beginning to feel distinctly nervous and asked Ascham how I should comport myself during the interview.

"Be extremely courteous, but don't be afraid to speak out boldly — rather a balancing act, I know. The King takes to a man who speaks his mind — provided what he says doesn't clash with his own views. The one thing you must *not* do is contradict him. Ah — this looks like your curtain call. Best of luck."

A page approached and asked me to accompany him. I followed the lad down a passage and was shown into the audience room. My heart was thumping like a trip-hammer and I licked dry lips to moisten them.

The door of the adjoining Privy Chamber opened, and a fat old man, swaddled in a dressing-gown, his legs wrapped in bandages, shuffled into the audience room, supporting his bulk on two sticks.

Could this be he whose image I had looked upon with awe, a few moments before? I stared in shock and pity at this pathetic wreck — the once dazzling monarch who could joust and hunt all day, and dance all night. Then I noticed that the little eyes, sunk in the pouched and flabby face, glittered with shrewdness, and that something in the lumbering stance hinted at immense will-power. I thought of a sick old lion — but a lion whose claws could still rend, and whose cunning was unimpaired.

Coming to my senses, I quickly dropped to my knee.

"Ah, Wainwright — the Cambridge student," rumbled Henry. "Which College do you attend?"

"Gonville Hall, Your Grace."

"Gonville Hall? Then you'll know of Dr. Caius."

"Yes, indeed Your Grace. One of the College's most distinguished Fellows. He was my tutor when I first went up."

"Ha! You know friend Caius's views on Welshmen?"

Disaster! I went hot and cold, remembering how Caius was famous for his dislike of the Welsh. And Henry's father has been descended from the ap Tidawrs of Gwynedd; they didn't come more Welsh than that.

"But we don't hold it against him," went on Henry, and I went limp with relief. "A brilliant fellow Caius. It's been our pleasure to command that he presently give lectures to the Surgeons of London. Strange," he went on in musing tones, "how our most trusted servants — Gardiner, Paget, Ascham and now yourself, are all men from Colleges in or off the same street as our new College of Trinity. There must be something in the air of that street that breeds loyal servants of the Crown. And there was never a time when the Crown had more need of loyal service than now — assuming that Ascham's theory is correct. An excellent fellow Ascham, but we wonder if too much Greek has addled his wits a trifle. A gun that spews bullets like water from a fountain! You

38

bring a fresh mind to this proposition, friend Wainwright. Do you not think that Ascham's giving his imagination too free a rein perhaps?"

"No, your Grace," I replied, feeling whatever reservations I might have about Ascham's theory dissolve, as I rallied to his defence. (Simultaneously, I recalled how Henry was notorious for playing off one person against another in order to test their views.) "It takes a bold as well as an intelligent man sometimes to recognize the truth, when that truth is too unpalatable or too strange to be acceptable by more cautious minds. As Your Grace himself has said:

'Every man has his free will;
The best ensue,
The worst eschew,
My mind shall be;
Virtue to use;
Vice to refuse,
Thus shall I use me.'"

Had I been presumptous in quoting these lines from Henry's own song 'Pastime with Good Company'? (By merest chance, Ascham and I had practised singing and playing it only two days previously, and the words still ran in my head.)

"Ha! We like it. You have a quick mind and a neat turn of phrase, my friend. You should have been a courtier. Very well — you have convinced us that Ascham is on to something, a great danger that threatens the safety of this realm. You have our blessing for your mission. Succeed, and you will have earned not only our thanks but England's. You may leave us now."

I left the audience chamber strangely moved and uplifted. (Yes me, Nick Wainwright — barfly, woman-chaser, cynic, idler, prankster; uplifted!) Now I understood what it was that made men like Ascham serve the King with such devoted loyalty. Transcending his ruthlessness and selfish scheming, Henry possessed a quality that made him truly great, an over-riding concern for the wellbeing of his realm, and a vision of that realm — an England strong, secure and free from the threat of interference or domination by any foreign power.

NO CHEESE ON FRIDAY

DURING THE return journey to Hampton Court, Ascham explained that all was now in train for my departure. After a light supper of mutton with galantine sauce, chicken and leeks, olive and cucumber salad, strawberry tarts, and a cheese table, washed down with claret, we went to St Jerome's Study as I called it, for a briefing session.

"There's a ship sailing from Tilbury in two days, bound for Sunderland," he announced. "The *Sir Bedivere*, of Portsmouth. You'll be on her. She's taking stores and reinforcements for Sir Thomas Wharton, the Warden of the English West March. From Sunderland, you'll travel with the reinforcements to Carlisle, picking up a detachment of the Bishop of Durham's troops en route. At Carlisle, you'll present yourself to Wharton with a letter of introduction. He'll see that you're escorted to Lochmaben Castle — that's in Dumfriesshire, in the Scottish West March, about as far north as they can take you and well clear of the worst area. That's Liddesdale — full of Elliots, Nixons, Laidlaws and Armstrongs, an unspeakable bunch of savages so intractable that they have to have their own special Warden or 'Keeper'. At present Lochmaben Castle is in our hands, but for how much longer is anybody's guess — the Scots seem to be getting their horns out again in the south-west.

"After you're dropped off at Lochmaben, you'll be on your own and will have to play things by ear. Your best bet, I imagine, would then be to head up Annandale, via Moffat to the height of land at the Devil's Beef Tub, when you'll be pretty well out of the combat zone. From there it's not too far to the Glasgow-Ayr-Lanark triangle. By sniffing around and examining straws in the wind, hopefully you'll discover if the secret weapon's being manufactured in that area. Stepped-up production or transport of raw materials, large concentrations of artisans, especially foreign ones, any unusual or hush-hush activity — these are the sorts of things to look out for; I don't have to spell out the details. By the way, our young Scots friend Walter Ker will be put over the Border with you; he's certainly earned his release."

Ascham grinned ruefully. "It's a pretty sketchy brief I'm afraid. If you get into trouble you'll be strictly on your own. The best I can do is give you the addresses of some 'safe houses'. He handed me a piece of paper on which was written the following:

Edinburgh
High Street, third house on the right from the
Netherbow Port, looking towards the Fleshmarket;
inscription on the ground floor lintel reads 'LUFE GOD
ABUFE AL AND YI NYCHTBOUR AS YI SELF',
Ask for John Mossman.

Lauder
Auldbiggin, a farm town with policies three miles north of
Lauder, on Leader Haughs where the Cleekhimin Burn
joins the Leader. Ask for the Laird, Dand Hoppringle.

Lesmahagow
Auchtygemmel Tower, one and a half miles north of the
town, on the right bank of the Nethan River. Ask for Sir
Oliver Douglas.

Midcalder
Calder House. Ask for Lord St John of Torphichen,
Preceptor and Prior of the Knights Hospitaller of St
John.

"Not much, I'm afraid," apologised Ascham, "but it's the best we can do. At least you'll have a few bolt-holes if the going gets rough."

"That Lord St John chap with the fancy titles sounds as though he carries a lot of clout."

"One of the Sandilands. They're pro-Reformation, which in Scotland generally means pro-English; friends of a fellow called

John Knox. Knox is thick with the Scots reformer Wishart, who's on our payroll by the way."

"I don't think much of the Scots' spelling," I said with a grin, "if that Edinburgh inscription's typical." I reached for the paper. "I'm to keep this?"

"Only for as long as it takes you to learn it by heart. Then destroy it. Security. Now here are a few more points you'll need to remember. If you make contact with anyone on that list, you're to say, 'The roads is gey clarty.' To which the reply will be — if your man's the genuine article, 'Come ben, ye'll be fair wabbit.' God, what a language! Come the Union, we'll have to teach them the King's English.

"If for any reason you have to contact me — something you must only do if it's absolutely necessary, write to me care of any of the three March Wardens. You'll refer to your mission by the Code name 'Operation Porcupine' — in legend, the Porcupine's supposed to be able to discharge its quills at an enemy from a distance. You'll refer to myself as 'Toxophilus'. Gardiner is 'Mr Stephens'. The King's Grace is 'The Old Man'."

"I don't believe it!"

"You'd better believe it. It's the King's own name for himself. *Your* name will be Jock Turnbull — Ecky's Jock, if anyone wants to know, to distinguish you from the hundreds of other Jock Turnbulls. Oh and by the way there'll be a written testimonial waiting for you at Carlisle, witnessed by the City Council and praising your quacksalvery to the skies. The fact that it's in England doesn't matter — Scots cross over the Border regularly, in spite of a war being on."

"Talking about quacksalvery — "

"Yes I know, we haven't done anything about it yet. Not to worry — what little there is to learn won't take long. In fact I've laid on someone for that purpose; you'll meet him tomorrow."

"You two have met, I believe," said Ascham with a smile, as he showed me into St Jerome's Study, where a spare, scholarly-looking figure in a dark gown stood by the fireplace. "I'll see you later," Ascham murmured, and slipped out.

The man's face, pallid beneath a superficial suntan, was familiar. Then I realised who it was — John Caius, Fellow of my College and my old tutor, before his departure for Italy six years before.

"Nicholas Wainwright!" The lined features broke into a smile. Caius advanced and clasped me by the shoulders. "It doesn't seem like six years since I stood 'in loco parentis' for you, old chap. Since I got back from Padua, I've been preparing a series of lectures to be delivered at the Barber-Surgeon's Hall in London. I've been pressed into service on behalf of my old sparring-partner Roger Ascham. (I recalled the famous row which had set Cambridge by the ears over the new pronunciation of Greek — Ascham pro, Caius anti.) It seems he wants me to help you pass yourself off as a quack physician." Caius shook his head and looked at me admonishingly. "What scrape have you got yourself into this time, Nicholas? All right — you needn't say anything; I'm not supposed to ask any questions. Well, I'll do what I can, though I warn you any help I can give you is not likely to amount to a great deal."

We chatted about Cambridge for a few minutes, then got down to business. "Look Nicholas," said Caius, "I won't beat about the bush. The amount of useful information I can give you, you could probably write on the back of a playing card."

"But — you're an M.D. of Padua, sir, " I protested. "The greatest medical centre in the world. Your commentaries on Galen, your lectures on the Sweating Sickness — they've made your name famous. They say you've studied under Montanus and the great Vesalius. Surely..."

"We've only begun to scratch the surface," said Caius gently. "Don't for goodness sake let on I told you this, but between ourselves the impressive front that the medical profession shows to the world — the College of Physicians, the Barber-Surgeons' Company, the Licenced Apothecaries, is really a facade to cover ignorance and confusion. We know so little, so hideously little. We study the Ancients and discover nothing for ourselves. Do you know what a physician has to master besides physiology? — grammar, rhetoric, logic, geometry and above all astronomy. Astronomy! We theorize that man is compounded of four humours — blood, phlegm, yellow and black bile, and that if these

43

humours became unbalanced we can put all to rights by a study of his urine, combined with blood-letting according to the phases of the moon." Caius paused and sighed. "I sometimes wonder if we aren't chasing moonbeams."

"The least regarded of us are the Surgeons, although they're the ones who get results — I sometimes think because their work is merely practical and not hampered by academic theories. There's a marvellous French army surgeon, Ambroise Paré — debarred from being a Physician because his Latin isn't up to scratch, would you believe? He's making tremendous advances in the treatment of wounds; I'll give his recipe for a salve for gun-shot injuries.

"Ascham tells me you'll be based in Scotland — well, at least that's better than Wales. Oddly enough, there's a little book, 'The Treasure of Poor Men' written by a Scot, that came out a few years ago. Not bad — been reprinted twice. I've a spare copy you can have."

When Caius left, some three hours later, I surveyed my stock-in-trade as a travelling quacksalver, with a mixture of relief and apprehension.

First, the Scots treatise, 'Ane gude Buke of Medicine callit the Treasure of Puir Men' (printed in London!), which contained such arcane information as; 'To purge the heid — juice of primrose, and milk. Blow through a pen into the nose.'

Secondly, a list of nostrums complied by Dr Caius from his own and other men's experience for alleviating minor ailments like boils, earache, sore throats, piles, cuts, sprains and so forth.

Thirdly, a treasure beyond price — a case of surgical instruments; scalpels, probes, scissors, calipers, suturing needles and gut, an amputating saw and, mutely eloquent, a mallet. ("I feel as though I'm giving gunpowder to a child," Caius had said. "No offence dear boy. Only use these things as a last resort in an emergency, or you'll end up killing rather than curing.")

After Caius's frank exposition, my sublime ignorance concerning all things medical no longer seemed quite such a massive handicap. Given a modicum of experience and luck, I felt I could probably hold my own. But how would I measure up if faced with even a minor operation — extracting a bullet, say? Well, I would cross that bridge if and when I had to.

The following day I was kitted up. I exchanged my 'civvies' for the following: thick kersey hose without feet and a loop to go under the instep, socks, linen shirt, loose tunic of close-woven worsted over which went a leather jerkin, boot-hose against chafing and half-boots of stout leather well hobnailed, a felt cap, and leather belt with purse and meat-knife in sheath attached — hardly the height of fashion but hard-wearing and practical. In addition, I was issued with a hooded cloak against foul weather, and several changes of shirts, undershirts, drawers, socks and hose. All this, plus my quacksalver gear (including Caius's prescriptions which had been made up by an apothecary) — was stuffed into a great wicker-framed pack. More personal effects — razor, soap, comb, a small mirror of burnished steel, a writing-compact (containing quills, pen-knife, paper, phial of ink), and a useful novelty, a tiny mariner's compass in a brass case, went into a leather satchel. A money-belt of kidskin, filled with rose-nobles and worn next to the skin, completed my outfit. As a parting gift, Ascham presented me with a steel wheel-lock pistol, plus powder and ammunition and a spanner to wind it up.

"It all goes on the bill," he said with a grin, as I tried to thank him for the beautiful weapon.

After lunch, who should roll up but Gardiner and Lamb to give me a send-off (or more likely, I thought, to check that I had been thoroughly licked into shape). As we were about to set out for the landing-stage, I realized that Walter Ker was conspicuous by his absence. A sudden conviction of foul play seized me. I halted and set down my pack. "Where's Ker?" I demanded.

"Yes, where *is* young Ker?" echoed Ascham. "I sent word for him to be brought here."

Gardiner and Lamb exchanged glances.

"We thought it — ah, politic, to have him returned to custody," said Gardiner smoothly. "For safe-keeping."

"After all, he's served his purpose," sneered Lamb. "What's one bloody Scot more or less?"

At this, I fairly lost my temper. "You two-faced bastards!" I

45

shouted. "That's all that matters to you, isn't it? Using people. Squeeze a man till he's dry then chuck him away — he's no more use. The idea, that by treating people decently you might actually get more out of them, never seems to occur to cold-blooded reptiles of your stamp. Well, this time you're hoist on your own petard. I'm not budging another step until Walter Ker shows up."

"For God's sake watch your tongue," Ascham hissed in my ear. "You can't talk to the King's Secretary like that."

"I just did," I said, feeling a surge of heady recklessness. This time, I had *them* by the short hairs and I wasn't going to let go in a hurry.

The three of them made quite a picture — Ascham, grim and worried, Gardiner, concerned but calculating, and Lamb, almost visibly swelling with rage — a comic sight, considering his lack of inches.

"Look, Wainwright," spluttered Lamb, "perhaps you don't fully realize your position. I'm warning you, if you don't immediately pick up that pack and —"

"Get lost," I snarled. "I'm warning *you* — either get Ker back here pronto, or the whole thing's off."

The three of them got into a huddle — Gardiner pursing his prim mouth and tut-tutting, Lamb fizzing and crackling like a damp firework, and Ascham — clearly almost as angry as I was, not pulling any punches with either of them.

At length Gardiner approached me. "Perhaps we have been a little — ah, hasty," he murmured with an oily smile. "I'll send a rider; with any luck, he'll overtake Ker's barge before it reaches London."

So back inside the palace we trooped; I had a good laugh to myself at making them sweat for a change, and my morale went up accordingly. Gardiner and Lamb disappeared, presumably to set in motion the machinery to recover Ker.

Ascham rounded on me. "Have you gone clean out of your mind?" he demanded. "All right — I agree that they behaved in a stupidly high-handed manner, but considering what's at stake, I think you might have spared us the schoolboy heroics. You'd better pray they can get Ker back in time for us to catch the *Sir*

Bedivere, before she sails. I wouldn't care to be in your shoes if they don't."

But they did, and Ascham, Ker and I dropped downriver in a prickling silence to London. Here we hired a fast barge with several strong oarsmen, who rowed us down to Tilbury — a dreary little place in the Essex mud-flats, with a fort and a ferry-service across the river to Gravesend. By this time the atmosphere had thawed to near-normal. Ker, somehow divining that I was the cause of his release, muttered a laconic, "Thankyou".

Scores of craft plied on the water or rode at anchor. One of these — a great warship, from the bold-looking knight painted on her stern must be the Sir Bedivere. Ascham saw us aboard. Before returning to his barge, he gripped me warmly by the hand. "Best of luck, Nicholas," he said, the banality of our farewell somehow underscoring the momentousness of the issue in which we were both caught up. "We never did have that archery match — something to look forward to when all this is over."

Ker and I stood at the bulwarks and watched as Ascham's barge rowed off into the sunset.

"Fur a Sassenach he's no sic a bad fella," remarked Ker.

"One of the best," I agreed.

"In the name o the wee man!" exclaimed Ker in disgust. "Say thon again."

"Sorry — 'yin o the best'," I corrected myself, remembering Ascham's golden rule about 'atmosphere'.

"H'excuse me — *sir*." The voice behind us was heavily sarcastic. We turned, to find ourselves confronted by a pock-marked ape of a man, the bosun who had received us aboard. With Ascham around, he had been reasonably respectful, but now that we were on our own, though clearly under orders to regard us as passengers, he obviously felt at liberty to treat a Scots bonnet laird and a travelling hawker with the contempt they merited.

Addressing Ker, he announced, "Cap'n says you're to take up quarters with the gentlemen. (He managed to make it sound as though they were a different species from Ker.) Abaft the mainmast." Then, turning to myself, "And you — you Scotch git. Leave that bloody dunnage on the deck. It'll be stowed below with

47

the stores. You'll not be needin' it till we drops the 'ook in Sunnerland dock. Get below ter the lower orlop. You can mess with Ned Halfhide's lot — they're one short."

"See youse aroond, pal," said Ker philosophically, and with a wave, headed aft carrying his portmanteau, as the bosun was clearly not about to order any of the seamen on deck to act as porter to a Scot.

"Just as well yer nancy-boy pal's berthin' topsides," the bosun leered. "'e'd not be safe below decks wivaht a cork."

With an effort, I controlled the rage that boiled up inside me. Ker might be a 'bonny callant' as the Scots would say, but I would have sworn he was no homosexual. However, there was no percentage in making an issue of it with this baboon. I could almost hear Ascham cautioning me; 'For God's sake Nicholas, you simply can't afford to get involved in any trouble.'

I clambered down a companionway, to find myself in a long, low room the width of the ship, flanked by huge cannon crouching in their carriages. It was like a scene from Dante's Inferno, with groups of soldiers getting noisily drunk and quarrelling among themselves or with the sailors. No one seemed to be concerned to impose any order to contain the confusion. By dint of asking, I was directed down more companionways to the lower orlop — a long dingy wooden cellar below the waterline, with tables ranged along the centre, and at the sides, curious net-like things some containing sleeping men, suspended between frames and the clamps supporting the deck beams.

I shoved through the press of close-packed bodies, asking for Ned Halfhide, and after being cursed or ignored half-a-dozen times, was eventually directed to a trestle table against the mainmast, where three men were seated on a bench. One of these was a big bald fellow with an outsize chin, another was a thin, furtive-eyed creature with projecting top incisors which gave him a distinctly rat-like appearance, while the third was a small yellow-skinned man with flat features, slanting eyes and jet-black hair done up in a pigtail. I had heard about Chinamen, but this was the first I had seen.

"I'm Ned 'alfhide," the big chap said in answer to my enquiry.

48

"And who might you be?"

I introduced myself and repeated the bosun's instructions.

"Shove over you two and make way for our new messmate, Jock Turnbull," said Halfhide. "You're just in time for supper mate." He rummaged in a box below the table and passed me a quart mug, plate and spoon of tin. "You'd best 'ave Sam Puffinthorpe's mess-kit. Poor sod cashed his tickets two days back — fell off the bleedin cross-trees and smashed his 'ead on the deck."

I sat down and Halfhide introduced me to the other two. "This skinny polecat's Aloysius Snipe, the lightest-fingered villain that ever crawled out of Alsatia; I should keep that satchel well buckled, mate. And our little yellow pal there's called Wong. Don't 'ave much to say for isself, but 'e's all right is our Wong, aint you me old China."

Snipe looked at the deck and snarled softly, while Wong beamed at me and shook hands with himself.

"Scotch aint yer?" said Halfhide sympathetically. "I shouldn't let it worry you too much. Pretty mixed bunch we've got aboard the old *Sir Bedivere*, what with all them bleedin mercenaries — Frogs, Wops, Krauts, even some bloomin Paddies and Greeks. Murdering scum. Do in their own grannies they would for the price of a pint. Pissed 'alf the time and fighting the other 'alf. Us Sir Bediveres are a pretty rough lot, I don't deny it, but we're lily-white angels compared to that crowd. Even the bleedin whores give the Sir Bed a wide berth, for Chryssakes. Ah, grub's up."

A group of youngsters carrying an assortment of buckets and pitchers was weaving through the throng, doling out rations at the tables. An object resembling a length of greyish-white board clattered on the table; some biscuit and butter was dumped on our plates and our mugs filled with beer.

"Bloody salt cod," snarled Snipe. "And no bleedin cheese. I'd forgot it were bleedin Friday."

The cod had the taste and texture of gritty cardboard and gave me a ferocious thirst, causing my quart to dwindle rapidly.

"She seems a braw ship," I commented in by broadest Jock Turnbull voice. I decided that I was quite enjoying my new persona.

"Finest in the King's Navy," affirmed Halfhide. "Built by Master

49

Shipwright, James Baker, no less. She's the best of a new type of ship — galleons they call them, long and low with a minimum amount of joinery work topsides. Not like the old *Mary Rose* with them bleedin great fore and after castles like ruddy packing cases stuck on top of 'er. The Sir Bed's fast and manoeuverable and can sail closer to the wind than any ship I know. Lateen sails on her mizzen and bonaventure masts, see. And with the metal she carries, she can deliver a broadside that'll blast a Frenchy out of the water at a furlong's range."

"But?" I prompted.

"You've seen it for yourself," growled Halfhide. "Discipline's shambolic. It's them bleedin mercenaries. They won't obey anyone except their own officers, who won't take orders from the Ship's Master. The Captain — Sir George Pettifer, 'e's doing his nut poor chap. 'e's a good bloke and a fine soldier — seen service in Ireland which can be pretty rough they say. But 'e's no seaman and the lads knows it. And 'e can't 'andle the soldiers. Know what 'e was 'eard calling to a captain in another ship? 'I 'ave the sort of scum I can't control.'"

"Sounds like we're all set for a happy trip," I observed brightly.

"You can say that again," snorted Halfhide, removing a fishbone from between two teeth. "There'll be trouble before we clear Flamborough Head. You mark my words."

"Plentee tlouble," affirmed Wong, grinning hugely as though this were something to look forward to. "Plentee fight, plentee men huht. Wong makee bettah. Plentee cumshaw."

"Isna there a barber-surgeon on board?" I asked, assuming Wong was referring to petty injuries as a result of shipboard violence.

"If you can call a Cornish butcher who's pickled worse'n a soused 'erring by that name — yes, I suppose there is. But 'e won't treat what 'e calls 'self-inflicted injuries'."

"But, with a respects to Wong..." I let the sentence trail away.

" 'e's just a higorant 'eathen Chink seaman," finished Halfhide. "Daresay 'e is, but e's a bleedin wonder with that little box of gold needles 'e's got. I've seen 'im shut up a bloke what's screaming in agony, by sticking a needle in 'is foot. Dunno 'ow 'e does it but 'e

50

runs rings round any bleedin doctor I've come across."

Supper over, Halfhide showed me the trick of climbing into one of the suspended nets.

" 'ammocks. New-fangled contraption from the Americas — the Dagoes learned about it from the Indians. Comfortable once you gets the 'ang of it. I should get your 'ead down mate while you've got a chance. Not like us poor sods who 'ave to go on watch in a minute. 'Ere, you'd better 'ave Same Puffinthorpe's blanket."

I took his advice and, after wedging my satchel below me, in case Snipe got any ideas, drifted off to sleep against a background of strange, but already almost familiar noises — curses in German, Italian and French, someone practising on a tabor pipe, the 'slap-slap' of water against the ship's sides, the clanging of a bell and the pounding of feet on companionways as the watch changed.

BAD JOSS

I WAS WAKENED by a rhythmic tramping on deck, accompanied by a wavering chant. I scrambled topsides to find the *Sir Bedivere* making ready for sea. Gangs of seamen were pushing round four long poles slotted into the capstan. Fascinated, I watched the procedure — the great drum wound up an endless messenger rope 'nipped' by lashings to the anchor cable. As messenger and cable came level with an open hatchway, a little 'nipper' undid the lashings, while the next section of cable coming through the hawsehole, was secured by more nippers, the section that had been untied being passed down through the hatch, to be coiled up below.

Up came the great dripping anchor; able seamen, directed by the bosun, caught it with ropes and lashed it immovably to the ship. The long-boat, skiff and joliwat towed us into mid-channel, and under topsails the *Sir Bedivere* began to gather way.

We glided slowly down the estuary and by early afternoon were off Shoeburyness.* Then, with all sails drawing, the *Sir Bedivere* headed out into the North Sea and was soon pitching in a steep green swell. I shall draw a veil over the next thirty hours or so, which passed in a state of comatose misery from seasickness. On Sunday evening, Halfhide coaxed me out of my hammock to gnaw a little salt beef washed down with beer. I kept it down and immediately began to feel a little better.

During Monday breakfast, (you've guessed it — salt beef, beer and biscuit), a smiling character made the rounds of the messes.

"Steward," Halfhide muttered to me. "Careful what you say mate."

Smiling Joe stopped at our mess. "Back to full strength, I see. A

This word is uncertain; there is a hole in the paper, probably gnawed by a mouse, so that we are left with S.......ss. The only other possible interpretation is Sheerness, but as the ship was about to head north, Shoeburyness seems more likely. (Transcriber)

little bird told me you were drawing rations for four again. Just thought I'd make sure there *was* a fourth. Can't be too careful, can we?"

"Jock Turnbull 'ere's taken the place of our fourth, who bought it, sir," said Halfhide shortly.

"Ah yes. The Lord giveth, etc. Welcome aboard Mr Burnpool. And where are you from, pray?"

"Cambridgeshire," I answered without thinking.

"Bloody liar," spat out Snipe. "You told us you was a bleedin Scotchman."

"Joke," I protested, grinning feebly, and cursing my carelessness. (If Ascham could have heard me!)

To my astonishment, I heard the word 'Liar' repeated loudly at the neighbouring messes. Within seconds, everyone on the lower orlop it seemed, was chanting in unison, 'Liar! Liar! Liar!'

"Bad luck," laughed Halfhide. "You've just elected yourself Swabber's Mate for the week. First to tell a whopper on a Monday gets the job. Ship's rule."

So I was proclaimed Liar at the mainmast, and entered on a state of servitude under the Swabber. He cleaned out the cabins but I had to do the really dirty jobs like swabbing out the bilges and the heads. I could scarcely object. The work was perfectly within my capacity to perform and my passenger status hardly granted me immunity. Also, the job had the advantage of giving me virtually the run of the ship without any questions being asked. Accordingly, I was able to have an occasional chat with Walter Ker, on the half-deck. (As a result of my little showdown on his behalf, his manner had become quite friendly, and we soon drifted into Christian name terms.)

"Ah'll no be sorry tae reach Sunderland," confided Wattie. "This ship's a fair madhoose. Thae sodgers is rinnin wild an seemingly naebody can keep them in order. The madness is spreadin amang the sailors as weel."

"How d'ye mean?"

"Next time ye're forrit, hae a keek at the bowsprit an ye'll see for yeirsel. Ah've a feelin things could turn ugly. If they do, it's best the twa o us stick thegither. At the stairt o trouble, meet me here on the hauf-deck."

I got the feeling that Wattie's premonition might not be unfounded. The atmosphere of dissension on the ship became almost palpable, like the air before a thunderstorm. The mercenaries, with nothing to do except gamble and quarrel, got on the sailors' nerves. One or two incipient fights flared up; steel was drawn and injury or worse avoided, only by the speedy intervention of the mate and the bosun who broke up the proceedings with fist and marlinspike.

The seamen expressed their resentment by becoming slack and unruly. This led to Draconian counter-measures to stop the rot. Following up Wattie's injunction, I went to have a look at the bowsprit; suspended from it was a basket containing a sailor. It transpired he had been caught sleeping on watch four times, and had incurred the penalty — to be put in the basket with a can of beer, a loaf of bread, and a sharp knife, to choose between cutting himself into the sea or slowly dying of thirst and starvation.

Presiding unhappily over this explosive situation was the Captain, Sir George Pettifer. I sometimes caught a glimpse of him among his gentlemen on the quarter-deck, his fine face lined with the strain of trying to cope with a situation that was beyond his powers.

The one bright spot in the set-up was the ship herself. A superb sailer, she made steady headway, tacking into a stiff nor'-easter that would have stopped a less seaworthy vessel or piled her up on the lee shore.

Off the Humber, the wind dropped suddenly, dying away to a light breeze. A great bank of fog rolled down from the Dogger, enveloping everything in a fluffy white blanket. The circle of visibility contracted, until you could scarcely see the forecastle from the half-deck. Sounds became distorted, at times so muffled as to be scarcely audible, at others unnaturally loud; a shouted order became a whisper, the squealing of a block sounded like the din of a brewer's sledge on the cobbles. A queer mood of restraint shot through with tension, seemed to grip the ship's company, men conversing almost in whispers, as though embarrassed to speak aloud. The cries of the sailor in the basket, and the chanting of the leadsman as the ship threaded a passage through the shoals and sandbanks of that dangerous coast, provided a nerve-shredding accompaniment to work topside.

Once, when I was emptying a bucket of urine into one of the half-barrels chained to the side (for a fire-precaution), a stay parted, knocking Wong overboard. I rushed to the bulwarks; miraculously, Wong had managed to grab the broken end and was being towed through the water. Grabbing the rope, I hauled him in hand over hand, like a fish on a line.

When finally he stood dripping on the deck, to my surprise he did not seem particularly pleased or grateful.

"Bad Joss to save man's life," he lectured me through chattering teeth. "Now you lesponsible foh Wong."

Partly to clear the debt he seemed to feel he owed me, he insisted on presenting me with his case of golden needles and laying on a course of instruction to go with them. "You plopah doctah." (If only he knew!)

From Wong's broken English, helped out by gesticulations, I gathered that the basic idea behind Chinese medicine was that in a healthy organism there was a continual circulation of energy. Illness could be defined as a derangement of this circulation, causing a deficiency or a disturbing excess of this life-force. Puncturing the skin with needles could redirect and normalize the flow of energy. This was possible because the limbs, trunk and head were lined with invisible 'meridians' related to the organs of the body and on which were located certain peculiarly sensitive points. A needle inserted at one of these points, would exert an influence on the organ related to the meridian on which that point lay. By pricking a number of carefully selected points, the physician could re-establish the normal circulation of 'ch'i' (the flow of energy) and bring the patient back to health.

I found this pretty hard to take at first. Superficially, it had some resemblance to the 'equilibrium of humours' holistic approach of conservative western Medicine, which Dr Caius had quietly de-bunked in favour of treating diseased organs on an individual basis. However, the testimony of several of Wong's shipmates, who swore that he had cured them of a variety of ailments ranging from lumbago and sciatica to bronchitis and asthma, was certainly impressive.

After two days' encapsulation in eerie whiteness, the fog vanished as suddenly as it had come. I was emptying slop buckets over the side of the waist, when the wind rose, the vapour wreaths shredded and dissolved and the sun shone forth bright and clear on a sparkling sea with the great cliffs of Flamborough Head away to port. A sight to gladden the heart on this first day of May, except for just one thing — a hostile flotilla two miles to the north-east, two great carracks, Scottish by their Saltire flags, and two galleasses streaming the French oriflamme.

Almost as soon as I had noticed them, they began to wear round with the obvious intention of intercepting us.

On board the *Sir Bedivere*, trumpets brayed and drums rattled for battle stations. I felt my pulses begin to race. Surely Sir George wasn't going to take on four ships of the enemy! His business was to deliver troops, not pick unnecessary fights, I'd have thought. With her speed, the *Sir Bedivere* ought to be able to give them the slip by turning tail, then resume her course when she had lost them. But whatever the reason — a desire to patch up his crumbling authority by a successful engagement, perhaps just a soldier's dislike of running away from a challenge, the *Sir Bedivere* held on her course, while the four enemy ships bore down, the galleasses looking like monstrous water-beetles, with their banks of oars flashing in the sun.

Topsides on *Sir Bedivere*, pandemonium reigned supreme. Cursing and struggling into their harness, soldiers in half-armour crowded into the waist, while archers and hackbutters scrambled onto the fore and after castles, trumpets screeching all the while to add to the confusion. Gunports popped open along the side, and with a prodigious rumbling of carriages from below, out slid a double row of cannon.

Although no expert in these matters, I think the *Sir Bedivere* with her great armament and sailing powers might have actually seen off the opposition, if discipline had been sound. And at first, things did go well for us.

Sir Bedivere's side swung round to face the nearest galleass, now less than a quarter of a mile away. Orange flashes rippled along her flank and a tremendous crash hammered my eardrums. The wind whipped away the gunsmoke to show a line of fountains subsiding just short of the galleass. A second broadside created spectacular havoc. Down came the top hamper with an audible crash; several cannon balls skittering along the surface, snapped off the oars on her port side like twigs. A ragged cheer rose from our people. The breech-chambers of *Sir Bedivere*'s anti-personell deck guns were loaded with iron dice or canisters of sharp flints, archers nocked arrows to bowstrings and hackbutters primed their weapons.

We closed to a hundred yards ... eighty ... fifty ... A storm of destruction burst on the disabled Frenchman. Down went crew and soldiers in heaps — even those in armour, the shot and clothyard shafts punching through tempered steel as though it were cardboard. The galley slaves, manacled to the benches, died in windrows where they sat. Screams and shouts blended with the hum of bowstrings, the hiss of arrows and the crashing of shots, into one appalling cacophony of death.

The *Sir Bedivere* began to wear round in order to discharge her port broadside at the other galleass, which having witnessed the fate of her companion, was churning up the sea with its oars in a frantic effort to turn around and escape. (A fluke shot from her stern chaser knocked the basket at our bowsprit into smithereens, ending the misery of the condemned sailor.)

The *Sir Bedivere* was halfway through the turn when a sudden gust struck her, causing her to heel sharply. Perhaps the sails were clumsily handled; perhaps the mass of men, many in armour, who crowded her upper works, made her top-heavy. Certainly, the gun-crews below must have neglected to close the starboard gunports, causing her to take in water. Whatever the reason, a perfectly standard manoeuvre went disastrously wrong.

Suddenly, terrifyingly, the heel became a list. With a stab of incredulous horror, I realized that the *Sir Bedivere* was beginning to roll over ...

As I instinctively grabbed onto the bulwarks, there flashed into my mind Wattie Ker's injunction to meet him on the half-deck. In the milling, sliding tangle of bodies, that was of course impossible, but I glanced up at the half-deck hoping desperately to catch a glimpse of him. Yes — there he was in the shrouds, waving frantically. Above the yells and curses, I could just hear his shouted message — "Clim ontae her side as she coups, then soom awa afore ye get sookit doon."

Numbly, I found myself obeying Wattie. I swung myself over the bulwarks and ran down the turning side, past the gaping gunports now looking to the sky, through which issued a blood-curdling babel of yells, over the bottom timbers slimy with weed, onto the mighty barnacle-encrusted keel. Then I was in the sea and striking out with all my strength to get clear of the doomed vessel.

Within seconds, my waterlogged clothes plus my satchel and money-belt began to pull me under. I began to thresh wildly. Then a voice sounded in my ear; "Turn on yeir back an dinna struggle."

Fighting panic, I did as I was told and found my chin gripped from below in cupped hands. Holding me from behind, Wattie kicked steadily away from the capsizing *Sir Bedivere*. From my prone position, I saw the end. Men were plunging by scores into the sea, those in armour sinking like stones. As the vast hull settled on its side, the shrieking from the hundreds trapped below suddenly cut out. For a few seconds she lay horizontal, then with a foaming swirl disappeared beneath the waves, leaving a gigantic crater boiling in the sea. The undertow plucked at us savagely, but we fought it and managed to stay afloat.

Flotsam bobbed up from the depths. We reached a spar and clung to it. The unharmed galleass came nosing among the wreckage.

"If ye ken ony o yon Frog lingo, ye'd best tell them we're Scottish," Wattie said in my ear.

Oars rising and falling like machinery, the galleass bore swiftly down on us. A soldier in the bows raised his caliver.

"Ne tirez pas!" I yelled. "Nous sommes Ecossais."

The soldier hesitated, turned and called to someone behind him. The galleass backed water and a rope was thrown. Seconds later we were aboard, water cascading from us onto her deck. I gagged at an appalling musky stench that filled the ship — the smell of the galley-slaves, I realized, just before being violently sick over the side.

'THE ROADS IS GEY CLARTY'

WATTIE AND I were transferred to one of the Scottish carracks, the *Sir Andrew Wood* for interrogation. My pulse-rate went up steeply but all went without a hitch, Wattie relating the plain facts of his own story with appropriate omissions, his only embellishment being his description of myself. I was impressed by this taken in the same skirmish as himself. I was impressed by this display of what an accomplished fabricator the Borderer is.

Once again, Wattie stayed topsides with the gentlemen, while I was relegated to the lower deck; we agreed before parting to join forces at Leith, whither the flotilla was bound.

My relief at surviving the sinking of the *Sir Bedivere* was tempered with dismay concerning my present predicament. I took stock in the way that Ascham had taught me — assess, plan, act. First, the debit side: instead of creeping into Scotland by way of her soft underbelly, with a friendly army of occupation guarding my rear, I was going to be dumped in the enemy heartland, on the opposite side of the country to the one I wanted to be in. All my quacksalver gear, to say nothing of my spare clothing was at the bottom of the North Sea. On the credit side, I was unharmed, my cover was intact, I still had my precious money-belt and satchel containing my personal belongings (Ascham's pistol I had carefully cleaned and dried), which now included poor Wong's case of golden needles — though I was sceptical about their usefulness. Also, Leith was only a stone's throw from Edinburgh where one of my 'safe houses' was.

So much for Assessment. Planning and Action would have to wait until 'the situation developed' to use another Aschamism.

Two days later, just as the sun was rising, we sailed past a great bun-shaped crag called the Bass Rock, into the Firth of Forth. To port, stretched a rich coastal plain studded with settlements, beyond which undulated a long range of hills — the Lammermuirs, I was informed by a burly seaman, who appeared beside me at the bulwarks.

"Aye — it's a braw sicht fae the deck o a ship," the sailor went on, "but if ye were ashore it wadnae look sae bonny. Ah'm fae Aberlady — thon's the port o Haddington, so Ah ken. Yon bugger Hertford — him that brunt Embro an Leith last year, ken whit he did on the wye back tae Berwick? Dang doon Lord Seton's muckle hoose at Preston, forbye howkin up a his orchards wi their bonny wee temples an bells, he wis sae prood o. Tranent, Haddington, Dunbar — Christ man, whit a hammerin they took. An the ferms an wee toons — Stevenston, Traprain, Kirklandhill, Hedderwick, Belton, an a, naethin left forbye a ruckle o blackened stanes. Bluidy English." He spat expressively over the side. "Hertford even left a force o cavalry ahint him, tae mind us Scots whae's the Master Race. So if ye're fur Embro lad, ye'll hae tae jine wi a pairty that's got an airmed escort, when we dock at Leith."

That port presented a dismal sight as we approached the harbour — every other building a gutted shell it seemed, and the pier a row of blackened stakes showing like rotten teeth above the water, so that those landing had to queue up to be ferried ashore in boats.

Reunited, Wattie and I were fortunate enough to find a large body of merchants and tradesmen bound for Edinburgh, assembling at Ballantyne's Brig, preparatory to running the gauntlet of Hertford's Riders.

Wattie told me he intended to put up at relatives in the fashionable Cowgate, before heading south for his own Border country.

Our party hurried up the road joining Edinburgh and Leith, past the village of Pilrig and a hill called the Calton, without encountering the dreaded Riders. Suddenly, there was Edinburgh on the other side of a shallow valley containing a loch — a long stone town running down a ridge that sloped from a great castle perched high on a rock, to a church and palace at the foot of a massive, craggy hill.

"Yon's St Giles Kirk," said Wattie with a proprietal air, pointing out a lantern spire that towered above the close-packed buildings.

"I thought — sorry 'thocht', that Hertford was supposed to have burned Edinburgh," I said in surprise. "There doesn't seem much sign of it."

"Aye — ye could hae fuled me," agreed Wattie, also nonplussed. "He disna seem tae hae made a verra guid job o't."

We passed the imposing church of Holy Trinity by the Nor Loch and entered Edinburgh by the Netherbow Port — a great gateway in the City Wall, separating the High Street from its continuation, the suburb of the Canongate.

"'Kingsway' — that's whit they're cryin it noo." Wattie gestured grandly up the street, splendidly paved with square blocks, and flanked by stone houses with crow-stepped gables and some with outside stairs. Much of the stonework was fire-blackened, contrasting with the roofs of tile and thatch, which for the most part looked rawly new.

"It's easy tae see whit happened," laughed Wattie. "When Ah wis last in Embro Ah mind the hooses a had wudden fronts — like thon yin ower there. When the English claimed they'd brunt Embro, a they'd done wis burn the roofs an they bit screens."

I suddenly realized that we had come to the parting of the ways. I held out my hand. "Well Wattie — this is whaur we split, I guess." I added lamely, "See you."

"In the name o the wee man!" exclaimed Wattie, shaking his head disgustedly. "Whiles Ah think you English is no real. Here's the twa o us been through hell an high water, and a youse can say is 'See you.' Ah'm Scots an ye're English, but Ah'd like tae think we wis freens. Ye'll look me up the morn's morn. Chap at the door o Sir Andrew Ker in the Coogate. Nine o clock'll dae fine. Nae excuses mind. Ye'll no can miss the hoose — next tae Cardinal Beaton's an a-body kens thon. Jist yin thing; it wadna dae fur ye tae come as Jock Trummle the travellin leech. How's aboot 'John Turnbull o Clovenshaws'?"

We shook hands warmly. "I'll be there Wattie."

Punching me on the arm, Wattie waved and strolled off along the crown of the causeway. Heads among the crowd turned to look admiringly at the slim, handsome lad who carried himself with such grace and assurance.

Now for John Mossman. 'Third on the right from the Netherbow Port looking towards the Fleshmarket,' I recited to myself. Surely that must be it on the opposite side of the street —

61

the one with wooden facings that Wattie had pointed out, a substantial house projecting into the roadway. Yes — there was that atrociously spelt logo along the lintel; 'LUFE GOD ABUFE AL AND YI NYCHTBOUR AS YI SELF'.

I crossed the road to a fine stone doorway opening onto the street. Looking in vain for a door-knocker, I rattled the ring enclosing a twisted iron bar — or 'rispit the tirlin pin' as I discovered later the phrase went.

A pretty blonde head popped through a hole in the boarding above me, and disappeared again.

A few seconds later, the door was opened by the owner of the head, a strapping maid with a mass of fair curls, who looked disdainfully at my scruffy appearance.

"Is the Maister in?"

"Ah whit if he is? Whit wad the Maister be wantin wi a gangrel body like yeirsel?"

"Just tell him Jock Turnbull would like a word wi him."

"Huh! Bide there." The door slammed in my face, to be re-opened after a few seconds.

"Ye're tae come in," said the maid, a trifle more civilly.

I entered what, from the iron-bound strong boxes, brass scales and baize-covered table, seemed to be a jeweller's shop. An alert-looking man with nutcracker jaws and high cheekbones, and wearing the old-fashioned long gown of a merchant, rose from behind the table and confronted me.

"Weel, whit is't ye want? Ye've been traivellin, by the look o ye." His gimlety black eyes seemed to weigh me up and find me wanting.

"Aye — the roads is gey clarty," I replied, feeling my confidence leaking away through my boot soles. Surely this brisk businessman couldn't be an agent in English pay? Ascham must have made a hideous mistake.

"Is tha' a fact? Come ben, ye'll be fair wabbit."

Weak with relief, I followed Mossman through the back of the shop and up a wheel stair into a pleasant room with panelled walls and painted ceiling (one of whose motifs represented a nude God with a distinct erection! — a surprising detail to find in this solidly respectable establishment.) It was all a bit dim and religious, as the

62

late afternoon sunlight could only penetrate through circular peepholes in the outside boarding which screened the window spaces.

Waving me onto a settle beside the fine tiled fireplace, Mossman rummaged in a cupboard and produced a flask and two red Venetian glass goblets. Pouring a clear liquid, he passed me a glass.

"Whisky," said Mossman with a wink. "Ah get it under the coonter fae the barber-surgeons, they bein the only boys as is allooed tae mak it. Beats yeir French claret ony day."

Innocently, I took a generous swallow — and gagged, as the fiery spirit scorched my throat. I began to launch into an explanation of my presence, but Mossman cut me short. "Haud on, lad. Dinna say ony mair. As far's ah'm concerned, ye're Jock Trummle — a traivellin quack fae the Borders. Ye can bide here at yeir pleasure; cash an gear — it's yeirs fur the askin. Onythin else, Ah dinna want tae ken." He smiled engagingly. "Ye look as though ye could dae wi a bath an a guid nicht's sleep. Jessie'll syne they clarty duds ye're wearin. The morn's Friday — the Grey Friars' flea-market'll be open. First thing, Ah'll send Jessie doon tae get ye some dacent second-hand claes. Ye'll need spare yins an gettin a tailor tae rin ye up a suit'll tak ower lang. 'sides, id wadna dae fur Jock Trummle tae be ower kenspeckle."

Despite his reluctance to get involved, when I pressed him Mossman agreed to have word sent to Ascham that I was safe (otherwise he must assume that I had gone down with the *Sir Bedivere*, when the news reached him) — by what means I couldn't begin to guess, and about which I dared not ask. A great weight seemed to slide from me as I followed Jessie downstairs to the kitchen for my bath.

FLOS UNGUENTORUM

NEXT MORNING, deliciously rested after a night in a comfortable bed (set into the wall after the curious custom of the Scots), and clad in respectable cast-offs, I was served breakfast of porridge, herring and ale by Jessie, in the kitchen (underlining the fact that my official status in the Mossman household was with the hoi poloi, I reflected sourly). Jessie's manner had thawed to the extent that she didn't actually bang the plates down in front of me. (I decided reluctantly that this improvement was unconnected with my bath the previous afternoon. I'd sat in a wooden tub while Jessie — quite unconcerned, had heated pails of water and poured them in; if you think that's a recipe for a turn-on, take my word for it, it isn't.)

"The Maister'll see ye this efternin at fower," said Jessie, clearing the table and eluding a hand which was beginning a flanking movement towards her waist. "If ye've naethin better tae dae, awa up tae the Luckenbooths an get's ma messages."

Armed with a shopping list and a purse of small change, I set off up the High Street, my height and decent garb (I would pass for a respectable tradesman) allowing me to keep to the 'croon o the causey' as the Scots put it, out of the piled-up filth at the sides where dogs and pigs rootled.

The Luckenbooths (locked booths) turned out to be a vast tatty tenement of shops built, incredibly, right in front of St Giles Kirk and separated from it by a narrow lane, appropriately named 'Stinking Style'. Wrestling with computations in the unfamiliar coinage, I eventually finished getting the 'messages'. Dropping them off at Mossman's, I cut down Blackfriar's Wynd to the Cowgate.

A bath, a good night's sleep, clean clothes and a full stomach, had done wonders for my morale and my mission now looked more like an exciting challenge than a desperate gamble. Now that I had a base (albeit a temporary one), I could re-equip myself and decide on the next step, or 'regroup prior to implementation of Phase Two' as Ascham would have put it.

Reaching the house of Sir Andrew Ker, I suddenly became self-conscious about my dowdy outfit, which I thought 'John Turnbull of Clovenshaws' wouldn't be seen dead in. But I needn't have worried. Sir Andrew turned out to be an absent-minded dotard in fustian whose sole interest was keeping bees. Apart from Wattie, the only other inhabitants of the rambling house were elderly menservants — all superannuated veterans of ancient campaigns like Flodden or the Ill Raid, and all it seemed with bits of their anatomy missing. There was Fingerless Will, Nebless Tam, Half-lugs Sim, even one Tail-less Clem, poor chap.

Against this collection of battered old crows, Wattie blazed like a resplendent peacock. Clad in the height of fashion, his slenderness masked by layers of loose upper garments — shirts, doublet, jacket, and short gown with puffed shoulders, he presented a silhouette that was massive and thrusting; the bulky torso carried upon hose-encased legs freed for movement, was the very image of virility. A flat plumed cap, sword and dagger completed his outfit.

"Wow!" I exclaimed, shielding my eyes as though blinded by this magnificence.

"We Kers like tae ruffle it a bit, when we're in Toon," said Wattie carelessly. "Come on, Ah'll show ye the sichts."

We strolled up the Cowgate, Wattie airily pointing out the houses of the rich and famous — the Earl of Buchan, Lady Borthwick, Sir Thomas Tod, et al. (I was secretly tickled to note one or two blemishes in Wattie's finery that rather spoiled the effect — a darn in his hose, an inexpertly-mended tear.) We passed an old folk's home with chapel attached, where workmen under the supervision of a sharp-tongued old harridan, were repairing damage to the roof. A chanting of bedesmen from inside, stirred far-from-nostalgic memories of Ely.

"Mistress MacQueen an her Magdalen Chapel," said Wattie. "Finished last year jist in time fur Hertford's Raid."

"And just in time for the Reformation?" I suggested.

"Aye — maist like," replied Wattie sourly. "It's no here yet but it's comin. Geordie Wishart an thon wee hell-raiser fae Haddington John Knox, and their killjoy pals'll see tae that. So sing awa bedesmen while ye've the chance."

With evangelising zeal, Wattie proceeded to drag me round the City till my feet ached and my head swam. I was shown the Grassmarket with St David's Tower in the Castle looming high above, the monasteries of the Grey and the Black Friars, the armbone of St Giles in its jewelled reliquary, the Flodden Wall with its gates or Ports, the Girth of Holyrood — the huge sanctuary in Abbey Strand, the Abbey itself and the Palace, still showing the scars of Hertford's Raid.

A pause for refreshment (pies and ale at an inn, which I paid for, Wattie suddenly discovering that he had left his purse at home), was followed by a hard game of tennis at the court adjoining the Abbey Watergate. Then it was time for me to return to Mossman's.

In the panelled chamber with the painted ceiling, I outlined my needs to Mossman over a working dinner of beef, pork, mutton, and duck, followed by jelly and washed down with Rhenish. ("Eatin wi the Maister upstairs noo, are we?" Jessie had snapped, seemingly put out by my fluctuating social status.) Basically, I required replacements for my quacksalver gear and some sort of permit, to do duty for my testimonial from the Carlisle City Council, which I wouldn't now be calling to collect.

"Nae problem," said Mossman. "The Royal College o Surgeons is gettin a wee bit stroppy aboot unauthorized practitioners, an is tryin tae get the authorities tae clamp doon on them. But there's wyes an means if ye ken the richt fowk. There's a remarkable Spanish fella bidin in Toon the noo. Cassanate — trained in Besancon an at present the Archbishop o St. Andrews' personal physician. Ah'll get ye an introduction. If he taks tae ye, he'll can get the Privy Cooncil tae gie ye a licence; he's weel in wi the high heid yins — Arran, Argyll, Huntly, Moray, Beaton, the hale clamjamfry. We may's weel tak a wee daunder tae wursels an see if he's at hame."

We found Cassanate in, at his lodgings in the West Bow. He was distinguished-looking in a dark spare way, charming, and — once he had satisfied himself that I was not a total incompetent, most helpful. He promised to speak to the Privy Council on my behalf, also to have some kit sent round.

This arrived the following forenoon by messenger. There was a copy of my old friend 'The Treasure of Puir Men', a parcel of expensive drugs — aloes, opium, petroleum, sulphur, benzoin, cardamoms, nux vomica, and senna, a long list of prescriptions carefully copied out from various sources such as Cheves's 'Lyber Graduum' (oil of roses for headache, willow bark for liver pain, ginger for purging viscous humours, etc.), including the recipe for Cassanate's own general-purpose salve, 'Flos Unguentorum'. In an accompanying letter, Cassanate assured me that he would be contacting the Privy Council on my behalf, without delay. (I couldn't help being a bit alarmed by this development, which was hardly consistent with my need to keep a low profile. I shuddered to think what Ascham would have said.)

A large pack purchased from a drunken pedlar in the Lawn-market, for I suspect several times its real value, completed my re-equipping. Mossman, being a jeweller and goldsmith, was able to change a few of my gold pieces into smaller Scottish denominations; outside the greater burghs he explained, I'd have had considerable difficulty in finding anyone wealthy enough to change 'yin o thae yella boys' as he put it.

In the afternoon I looked up Wattie, who took me out to the suburb of Greenside below the Calton to see a recent play by one Sir David Lindsay, 'Ane Satyre of the Thrie Estaitis'* in which the Establishment, the Church especially, came in for stick. (Once again I found myself paying; I didn't mind, for Wattie was good company, besides I could afford it — though Wattie wasn't to know that.) My Scots wasn't yet good enough for me to follow it all, but Wattie translated the key bits, and the steamily seductive Dame Sensuality kept my attention from wandering.

"On Monday morn Ah'm leavin fur the Borders," said Wattie, as we walked back to the Cowgate. "If ye're fur the Sooth yeirsel, whit say we gang thegither?"

I welcomed this suggestion for I had been secretly dreading the

*Written in the late 1530's, this famous play received its première in Linlithgow. Some modern scholars have stated that it had its first Edinburgh performance in 1554; Wainwright's comment proves that it was in fact performed nine years earlier. (transcriber)

prospect of striking out alone into Darkest Scotland. The nearest apex of the Glasgow-Ayr-Lanark triangle was Lanark, in a south-westerly direction from Edinburgh, which meant that I could probably do the first leg of the journey in Wattie's company.

"That's fine by me," I replied. "I'm for Clydesdale actually. Will you be going — er, 'gangin' that way?"

"Aye. As far's Biggar."

Then a snag occurred to me. "But of course ye'll be riding. I'll be on fit. Well, it wis a guid idea."

"Will ye listen tae him?" sighed Wattie. " 'You'll be riding. I'll be on foot.' In the name o the wee man! If Ah had but the yin cuddy, we'd ride an tie. It'll be an ill day fur the Kers if Uncle Andra canna gie's the lane o anither nag, forbye the yin that Nebless Tam'll be ridin."

"Well — if you're sure that's all right, then. Thanks. But why's Tam coming?"

Once again Wattie sighed, as though dealing with an obtuse child. "Where wis you drug up, onywye? A Ker disna ride wi-oot a servant."

Yes, and 'Alexander of Macedon and he that dressed his mules, when once dead both came to one,' I quoted to myself (from good old Marcus Aurelius), both nettled and amused by Wattie's aristocratic airs.

THE PLAGUE CHAPEL

THE FOLLOWING MORNING, I woke to find the Mossman household in a great tizzy, with Mossman himself being buckled into armour by a young son. Noticing my concerned expression he grinned and said, "Dinna worry — Hertford's no come back. The day's the first Sunday o May, when the toonsfolk bring hame the Summer. Jine the fun, lad." He winked at Jessie, busy preparing breakfast. "Jock here'll mak a grand jo fur ye."

Jessie bridled and 'humphed', but I was an old hand at reading the signs, and could tell that she liked the idea.

Before the procession started, I hurried down to the Cowgate to ask Wattie along.

"Whit — a Ker be 'Hail fellow well met' wi the toon keelies?" he sneered. "Nae wye."

Stung by my friend's snobbery, I returned to Mossman's, where the sight of Jessie in a red gown, close-fitting above the waist, flowing below, dissolved my irritation.

Drums beating, banners flying and cannon roaring, the citizens of Edinburgh marched down the High Street. There were garlanded horsemen, guisers, dancers, a boy bishop, and in the van, just in front of the Master of Ceremonies ('Robin Hood'), the wealthy Hammerman, with Mossman well to the fore, in full armour with their drums and banners.

Out through the Netherbow Port we wound, down St Mary's Wynd, past the Kirk of St Mary in the Field and away past the Burgh Loch and the nunnery of St Catherine of Siena to the Burgh Muir — a vast heath rolling away westwards from Arthur's Seat (the great hill above the Palace). Wattie could keep his blue blood and threadbare finery, I thought as I slipped an arm round Jessie's waist. With his looks and bearing, he could have had the pick of the girls on the Burgh Muir that beautiful first day of summer. I pictured him at Uncle Andrew's in the Cowgate, not wealthy enough to ruffle it in style with his peers, killing time by playing cards with the old man, with no other company but bees and decrepit veterans.

That celebration on the Burgh Muir seemed part carnival, part fair, part picnic. Hawkers, musicians, jugglers and acrobats, moved among the good-humoured crowds. (With such a vast number, many of them armed, there was no risk of Hertford's Riders turning up to spoil the fun.) Robin Hood, Little John and Co. (aristocrats all, so snubs to you, Wattie), decked out in mediaeval costume, presided benevolently over events — wrestling bouts, races, an archery contest, etc. Dances were organized — vigorous country ones, also, to my surprise the latest importations from the Continent, Branles, Pavanes and Saltarelles of Susato and Attaignant. Class divisions seemed to crumble, merchants, tradesmen and nobility all joining together to make up sets for the dances. I rather fancied myself as a demon of the dance-floor, but there was nothing I could teach Jessie in the way of steps or reverences.

After one particularly vigorous galliard, we decided it was time for a break and strolled off to find a quiet spot where we could relax. Time to give the old Wainwright technique — a slimy but effective combination of flattery, deference and opportunism, an airing. Aha, the very thing — a little chapel at the foot of Blackford Hill, well away from the main crowds.

"St Roques," murmured Jessie doubtfully. "They pit up pest-huts here when the plague comes tae Embro. There's burial pits a roon aboot." And she gave a little shudder — more of excitement than disgust, I decided.

It's a theory of mine, borne out by experience, that there's nothing like a hint of danger, or the presence of our bony friend of the scythe and hourglass, to put a woman in the mood. And a dash of sacrilege — like making your advances in a chapel, doesn't do any harm.

The chapel was dim and cool, a welcome contrast to the glare and warmth outside. We sat side by side on a stone pew along the wall. Now that we were alone for the first time (I didn't count Mossman's kitchen, where we had been encapsulated by a large household), I took stock of Jessie. Big, blonde and buxom — just as

70

I liked them. Spirited too, and with a hint of underlying passion which once aroused, might I suspected, prove pretty incendiary.

"Do ye come here often?" I said, striving for lightness, but the huskiness in my voice betraying my excitement. (Damn!)

"Oh Jock — ye're a fule." She giggled — shakily, I noticed. (Good.)

I lifted her hand, chapped and work-reddened in contrast to the creaminess of her complexion. (Her hands were her weak points — score there. Useless praising her obvious attractions; she'd have been complimented on her face and figure a thousand times.)

Murmuring endearments to her hand, I carried it to my lips and began tenderly to kiss each finger in turn. "Ye're awful nice Jock," she sighed, and leaned her head on my shoulder.

My lips left her hand and sought her mouth. She stiffened momentarily then yielded, clasping me strongly to her while our mouths locked hungrily.

This was the moment when the campaign was lost or won; while we still strained in a passionate kiss, my practised fingers flew to the fastenings of her gown. (Once stormed, these outer works were seldom retaken by the defenders.) Points, lacings, hooks and eyes popped apart, and my hands were gently fondling her breasts before she could regroup her forces and organize a resistance. To a silent count of ten my fingers described ever narrowing circles towards the poles of those magnificent globes ... two, one, zero. My fingers homed in on her nipples which instantly swelled erect; at the same moment, her murmured "No Jock" changed to a gasp of ecstasy. My mouth fastened on a nipple, freeing a hand to push up her gown and petticoat and make a sortie between her legs. Her vulva was already slippery; the little sentry guarding the entrance to her sally-port stood up straight and stiff as Herald Finger began a parley with him. Her breathing became a series of rhythmic pants, her fingers tore at my codpiece point ...

"Now Jock — now!" she yelled. We slid to the floor, her legs opened, and my triumphant vanguard entered the gate of her citadel. Violent spasms shook her body, triggering my own tumultuous release.

We surfaced slowly, smiling into each other's eyes. As we did our

71

clothes up, I found myself analysing my reaction and surprising myself by my findings. Invariably, at such a moment, I found myself mentally chalking up another score, while at the same time scheming a strategic retreat. Careful planning, a quick kill, and out — that was the Wainwright policy. With this girl, somehow, I felt differently. I found that I wanted to take her in my arms again and kiss her tenderly. Was I going soft? Could it be that Wainwright, who had borne a victorious lance in Cupid's tournament a score of times, was unhorsed at last? With a mixture of wry amusement and wondering tenderness, I embraced her.

"Oh Jock," she sighed happily, and snuggled against me.

The afternoon drifted past in an idyllic dream. Wrapped up in ourselves, we strolled on Blackford Hill and picnicked beside the Braid Burn on the cold chicken and white wine I'd brought in my satchel. Blissfully replete, we stretched out on the warm turf and dozed off ...

I was awakened by Jessie shaking me. Her eyes were wide with fright; she held a finger to her lips, then pointed over my shoulder. I turned my head. Fifty yards away, two soldiers in half-armour were watering their horses in the Braid Burn. Hertford's Riders! In my preoccupation with Jessie, I had allowed my awareness of the lurking menace of this mobile harrying force to slip to the back of my mind.

Clearly they hadn't seen us yet. But even as we started crawling towards a clump of trees, one of them raised his head and looked me full in the face.

In that frozen instant of time while we stared at each other, my mind registered inconsequent details — a copper rivet showing through the canvas covering of his brigandine, a splash of mud on one of his thigh-boots, the brutal mouth below a full moustache.

Assess, plan, act. Thank God for all those hours of punishing training under Martin. After the first shock, my mind began to work coolly and clearly. I reached under my shirt and unbuckled my money-belt; I swung it in my hand, testing its weight. Gold is heavier than lead. If I could time my swing right, I had a lethal weapon.

The soldier grinned and drew his sword, as did his companion —

a burly giant with a livid scar across one cheek.

"Oho — two fine yoong Scotch pullets for the ploocking," said Tash to Scarface, in a Lincolnshire accent. "We'll 'ave a right bit o' foon with this pair."

Slowly, they began to advance, Scarface inching round to the flank to cut off our retreat, an unnecessary move — Jessie wasn't going to be breaking any speed records in that gown.

"It's a right," I said to Jessie. "I ken what I'm doing. Stay behind me and keep out o the way." Suddenly my heart gave a leap as I remembered my pistol. "There's a loaded wheel-lock in my satchel," I whispered. "Get it out, plus its spanner and be ready to hand them to me."

By this time, Tash had halted a few feet away. The belt dangling in my hand clearly posed no threat as far as he was concerned.

"Aha!" He lunged with the blade, the point stabbing the air inches from the side of my face — a deliberate miss. Clearly, he intended having his 'bit o' foon' before going in for the kill.

I stood my ground, watching him carefully as he tensed himself for his next feint. As his sword-arm drove forward, my left foot lashed out, connecting with his wrist. There was a crack like a snapping branch, a howl of pain, and the sword flew from his dangling hand. Then my belt, with the full weight of its golden contents, slammed into his temple. He collapsed without a sound, his skull stove in like a cracked walnut.

All this had happened in seconds. I whirled round to take on Scarface; he stood stock-still, his mouth still widening in surprise. Suddenly a black hole appeared in his forehead and a crash hammered against my eardrums. Scarface's look of surprise petrified, he swayed then toppled face-first onto the ground. Where the back of his head had been, a ragged crater gaped.

I turned to see a white-faced Jessie holding the smoking wheel-lock with both hands.

"Good girl!" I exclaimed. "Oh ye bloody wonderful, marvellous girl." I flung my arms round her, holding her while she sobbed herself out against me. I was trembling like a leaf myself. The realization that I had just killed a fellow-Englishman and been party to the death of another, troubled me not one whit. The world was a

73

cleaner place without such scum.

We dragged the bodies into the clump of trees, and leaving the horses cropping the grass as if nothing had happened, returned to the little chapel.

"I didn't know ye could use a pistol," I said admiringly.

"Ah'm no jist a pretty face, ye ken," said Jessie with a tremulous smile. "The Maister whiles gets commissions tae decorate wheel-locks wi siller work. He's shown me how tae wind yin up an cock it." (What other things had he shown her? I wondered savagely. Then I realized that I was being irrationally jealous. Wainwright jealous! God, I really must be smitten.)

We fell to kissing and cuddling. In no time at all, we were making love with a frenzied urgency that left us both shaken.

Long after the crowds had paraded back to town carrying birch branches, as their ancestors had done from time immemorial, we set out from the chapel as the sun's last rays gilded the summit of Arthur's Seat. With dusk gathering, there was little risk that any more of Hertford's Riders would still be at large.

"How'll we get in?" I asked, not really bothered at the prospect of spending a night under the stars with Jessie. "The Ports'll be shut by now surely?"

"Dinna worry. On the nicht o bringin hame the Summer, the Keepers'll let's in nae bother. An even if they didna, there's a break in the Wa Leith Wynd we'll can clim ower."

"Mossman's going to dae his nut."

"Och, no him. He's an easy-gaun body, 'specially at the Passin tae the Wud."

And so, hand in hand, we strolled homeward. Near the Burgh Loch, with lights in a few late-abed Edinburgh households twinkling less than a mile ahead, we paused for a breather. We were in the middle of a long, long kiss, when I became aware of a faint creaking *above* me! At the same moment my nostrils caught a whiff of a dreadful carrion stench.

Breaking off, I glanced up. A few yards off was a walled enclosure from which rose a tall framework of beams. Suspended from the cross-ties, grisly things which had been men swayed gently in the evening breeze. I was thankful for the near-darkness which prevented me from making out the more gruesome details.

To my surprise, Jessie burst into a storm of weeping, and clutched me to her as if afraid that I was about to fly up into the air and join the grim assembly above us.

THE LEPER HOUSE

"COME ON," I soothed. "It's only a gibbet. They can't harm ye."

"Ah ken! D'ye tak me fur a bairn?"

"What is it then?"

"It's yeirsel Ah'm feared fur. Oh Jock — if onythin sud happen tae ye — . Ah dinna think Ah could bear it; no efter whit they did tae Davie. Och, Ah shouldna be sayin this . . ." Again, her body was racked by sobs.

Tactfully steering her away from that stark tree with its horrible fruit, I held her close until her sobbing ceased. Alarm bells were suddenly shrilling in my brain.

"Tell me," I said gently, allowing no hint of urgency to creep into my voice.

"Aweel — ye're no tae say ocht tae ony-yin aboot this, mind. Sax weeks lang syne a lad cried Davie Baxter cam fur tae see the Maister. Got up as a traivellin packman like yeirsel. A bonny lad forbye." She gave my waist a reassuring squeeze; "But no sae bonny as ma Jock.

"He wis aye speirin aboot sodgers' business — guns an siclike. He wis as much a packman as ye're a quacksalver. Ye needna worry — Ah'll no let on. Ah'm no supposed tae ken aboot the Maister's secret daeins, but Ah've een in ma heid an lugs forbye, an Ah canna help but pit twa an twa thegither."

"What about the guns?" I asked, trying to sound casual. Although outwardly calm (I think), inside I was torn by conflicting emotions — rage that Ascham had told me nothing about this predecessor who seemed to have come to a sticky end, fear that the 'safety' of my safe house might prove a snare and a delusion, and a sharp anxiety concerning Jessie lest she get embroiled in this murky and dangerous game.

"When he fand oot there wis an airmaments factory up at the Castle, he wis like a cat on a het griddle."

"Armaments factory!" I couldn't help exclaiming.

76

"Aye. A-body kens thon. Frenchies turnin oot brass cannon maistly. The Seivin Sisters that were tane tae Flodden back in the '13 wis wrocht there. Whiles ye canna sleep at nicht fur the duntin o the forges."

I felt my pulse-beat quicken. Perhaps 'Operation Porcupine' should be conducted here in Edinburgh, rather than in the Clydesdale Triangle.

"What happened to Davie?" I pressed gently.

"He went oot the yin forenin sayin he'd be back or nicht, but niver a sicht nor soond o him, though the Maister bad up till lang efter the shuttin o the Ports. Twa days later, he got rid o a Davie's gear that he'd left ahint him, in an unco hurry. He cautioned the hale hoose tae say naethin if ony-yin cam speirin, but this; a gaberlunzie-body had come chappin at the door an wis sent awa.

"Weel, three weeks on, Ah wis deliverin some broken meats tae the Leper Hoose ootside o the Wa, an there wis Davie ..." Her voice broke; she fought for composure for some seconds, then went on shakily, "Oh Jock — the things they'd done tae him. He wis sittin at the door soondin a clapper atween his stumps o palms — they'd cut aff his fingers. An they'd pit oot his een. He couldna speak — just mak mewlin soonds like a kitling. When he opened his mooth Ah saw fur why - he'd nae tongue. Whiles Ah think they'd cut it oot because he wouldna clype, fur naebody cam speirin at the hoose. It was pitifu, pitifu."

My scalp crawled as I thought of that mutilated wretch condemned to a living death among the lepers, more effectively shut off from human contact than if he'd been locked in the fastest cell of the Tolbooth. Far kinder to have killed him and be done.

"Was Davie — important, to you Jessie?"

"Och no. Ah liked him fine, ken. Whiles we'd hae a bit crack thegither, but thon wis a. Naethin like me an youse." And she gave me a quick hug.

"Where is this leper house?" I asked innocently.

"It's on the auld tiltyaird, forenent the Calton — " She broke off, then continued fiercely, "Ye'll no gang tae yon place, Jock Trummle. Promise me ye'll no gang."

That was in fact exactly what I did intend doing, but I managed to persuade her otherwise.

"Naebody but the Carmelites whae looks efter them is allooed inside o the hoose. An nane o the lepers can leave the hospital. Thon's the rules an the penalty's death fur ony-yin whit breaks them. Jist you mind thon, Jock Trummle."

I soothed away her fears with kisses, and we made our way back to Mossman's via the break in the Wall that Jessie had mentioned.

Leaving the door 'on the sneck', as the Scots say, I slipped into the deserted High Street. Retracing my way down Leith Wynd to the Wall, I clambered through the gap and followed the Wall to its end at Trinity College Kirk by the Nor Loch.

'The auld tiltyaird forenent the Calton.' What the hell did 'forenent' mean? I wondered as I cast around, trying to get my bearings. (Why couldn't the Scots learn to speak English?) In the event, I found the hospital without difficulty. At the north-east side of the Craigend Gate, just east of the road to Leith and in the shadow of the Calton, loomed an isolated building. This must surely be the leper house — the surrounding area was flat as a pancake, presumably the old tiltyard. As I approached the building, fear, which until then had lurked at the edges of my mind, now took full possession of it. The lateness of the hour, the loneliness, the stark shadows cast by the moonlight, created a strange unearthly atmosphere. This, combined with my knowledge of the consequences of being caught, and the horror which leprosy inspires, made my mouth dry out and my palms sweat as I tiptoed towards the hospital.

It was a substantial stone-built affair, the windows narrow slits — to lessen the risk of contagion I supposed, for the officiating Carmelites and for passers-by. I could feel my heart pounding as I rapped the door-nail.

Before the echoes died away, I heard a shuffling from inside. A flap in the door was lifted and a hoarse voice called, "Whae is't?"

"A friend o Davie Baxter."

The moonlight flashed on a pair of eyes which appeared behind the slit. "Ye're no yin o the Brithers." The voice was hard-edged with suspicion. "Whit is't ye want?"

"A word wi Davie Baxter. It's important that I see him."

"Man ye canna come in here. Wad ye see us a hangit?"

"Just a word," I persevered, trying to keep the desperation out of my voice. Just in time, I stopped myself from holding a gold coin up to the slit. Apart from the apalling security risk, what use would gold be to a leper? "Where's the harm? He canna have caught the disease yet, surely?"

"Whit if he hasna? Ye canna come in, Ah tell ye. Noo leave us."

"Wait," I pleaded. "Look — jist tell him I've a message from 'Toxophilus'".

A receding shuffle sounded from behind the door. Was the leper going to summon David Baxter? Or was he breaking off communication?

Seconds passed, then the footsteps approached again, accompanied by others. A key grated and the door swung open.

"Twa meenits."

I took this as an invitation and stepped inside. A stale mephitic odour filled my nostrils. By the moonlight which entered through the narrow windows and the momentarily open door, I made out that I was in a fairly large room with cots containing huddled figures ranged along the walls. The leper who had admitted me shut the door, but not before I had caught a moonlit glimpse of silvery webbed hands, and a dreadful head like a mouldering vegetable. Behind him was another figure only slightly less terrible, with fingerless stumps for hands and raw gaping sockets where his eyes had been. The other moved away, leaving the blind man and myself alone by the door.

"Look — just nod or shake your head in answer to my questions," I whispered. "You're David Baxter?"

Nod.

"I'm from Toxophilus. Did you find the Porcupine?"

Shake.

"Is it being made in the arms factory in the Castle?"

Shake.

I repeated the question, but again Baxter shook his head, more vigorously this time. I was slightly thrown by his denial; I think I had unconsciously begun to assume that Edinburgh Castle would prove to contain the Porcupine's lair.

Baxter leaned towards me. Gargling hisses issued from his cavernous mouth. Putting my ear close, I strained to catch his message. He repeated three aspirations — I cannot call them words, that sounded something like, "Haich — macha — hichoh." (The 'ch' was sounded as in Scottish 'loch').

He uttered the message a third time with obvious urgency.

"Yeir time's up," said the leper who had admitted me, and advanced towards the door.

The thought of seeing the creature at close quarters again was too much for my nerves, already strained to breaking-point. I opened the door and, I am ashamed to admit, fairly bolted from that place of horror. Drawing the night air deep into my lungs, as though to purge my system of any lingering effluvia from the leper house, I hurried back to the City Wall and returned to Mossman's without incident.

Slipping into my box-bed in the wall, I found myself enfolded by a pair of soft arms, a tear-wet face touched my cheek, then Jessie's hungry mouth fastened on mine.

CAULDSTANESLAP

WHEN IT CAME to leave-taking the following morning, I found that I was genuinely sorry to be going. I decided that this reaction was due to, a) my real fondness for Jessie (Wainwright bites the dust, I thought cynically), and b) exchanging the security of a congenial base for arduous travelling and unknown hazards.

"Cassanate sent this roond," said Mossman, handing me a scroll. "It's yeir licence fae the Privy Cooncil."

I unrolled the crackling parchment and read the following: 'To the Provest, Baillies and Consale of whatsamevir Burgh in oure realme of Scottelande in quilk oure weilbelufit JOHN TURNBULL may desire for to bide, forsameikil as thaforesayd JOHN is ane honeste and rycht skeely leeche, we charge that ye permitte the samyn to ministere to the sicke with salves alsoe to cut for the stane, cure ruptures, cataracts and pestilence, treat dystempers of wemin eftir birthand . . .', etc., etc.

Good old Cassanate! Armed with this (despite the hilarious spelling), my cover was rock-solid, enabling me to travel freely anywhere in the country.

Mossman pressed a small parcel into my hand. "Open it later Jock. Jist a bit knick-knack, but it'll mebbe come in usefu. Mind, it's no a-body can say they've somethin wis wrocht by the man whae made the Royal Croon o Scotland." He gripped my hand. "A the best, lad."

Jessie helped me on with my pack and accompanied me to the door. There, she fastened round my neck a good-luck charm on a chain, in the form of two joined hearts — a tawdry thing of pewter from the Luckenbooths, but more precious to me than finest gold. It is round my neck as I write this.

"A keepsake fae yeir Jessie," she said, and there was a catch in her voice. "Ye'll whiles think o me, Jock?"

"Look Jessie, when all this is over — " I began, but she cut me short.

81

"Wheesht," she said, choking back a sob, then hugging me. We kissed long and lovingly, then she broke away and ran inside the house.

I set off up the High Street. At the corner of Niddry's Wynd, I turned and looked back; the last I saw of her was a golden head framed in one of the peepholes of the wooden frontage.

At Uncle Andrew's all was astir against our departure. Two 'hobblers' — small hardy Border horses, had been provided for Wattie and myself, besides a mule to carry our baggage, and a scrawny hack for Nebless Tam. This worthy, as if his lack of a nose didn't make him conspicuous enough, was tricked out in an antique sallet that could have seen service at Flodden, and, in place of the usual quilted jack, a rusty corselet complete with shoulder pieces. A long lance, projecting from a holster attached to his mount's saddle, completed our escort's outfit. (Tam might look like something out of an ancient woodcut from Malory's Morte d'Arthur, but he had served in the famous Scots Guard in France, so presumably knew his business.)

As for Wattie, gone was the fashionable popinjay; he cut a workmanlike figure in long boots and jerkin, of buff leather.

Tam leading the mule, we rode out through the West Port, then headed south-west over the Burgh Muir, past the Napiers' tower of Merchiston to the village of Hailes, where the Water of Leith ran through a deep, wooded glen. Here, we watered our horses then, fortified by a draught of ale from a local tap-house, rode up into the lovely green range of the Pentland Hills.

Wattie was in good form, holding forth on his favourite topic — blue-blooded Scottish families: Scotts, Maxwells, Homes, Hepburns, Douglases, etc. ad nauseam. The subject bored me out of my skull, so uttering the occasional "really" or "you don't say?" to keep Wattie happy, I slipped into my own thoughts.

Mossman intrigued and puzzled me. Why should a wealthy and respected goldsmith, and a Scot to boot, harbour English spies? Of course, the Scots were notoriously divided regarding what was best for their own country, and many genuinely believed that union with England was in Scotland's best interests. Perhaps Mossman subscribed to this doctrine; perhaps he got a kick out of playing a dangerous double game. I couldn't believe that a man of his affluence was in it for the money.

Recalling his present, I took the parcel from my satchel and undid the wrappings. Inside, was a beautifully-made silver skull that gave forth a ticking sound. Undoing a catch, I pushed back the brain-pan to disclose a miniature clock-face! The thing was one of the new portable timepieces, or 'Nuremburg Eggs' as they were called. Delightedly, I slipped it inside my tunic; whatever kind of man Mossman might be — schemer, traitor, patriot, he was a warm-hearted and a generous one.

I chewed over David Baxter's enigmatic utterances. What sounds would be affected by his lacking a tongue? Trying not to use my tongue, I said the alphabet to myself, and found that I was wholly or partially unable to pronounce the following: d, g, j, k, l, n, q, r, s, t, x. The first word — 'haich' could be intended for: Haig (the surname?), hake, hail, hale, hare, hear, here, hat, hate?

The second word — 'Macha' didn't seem to translate into anything that made sense: mada, maga, maja, and so on. The meaning of the third word — 'Hichoh' was even more elusive. All I could be certain of was that it consisted of two syllables, the first containing the vowel sound 'i' (as in 'kiss'), the second 'o' (as in 'long' or 'bawd'). I juggled with endless combinations, the most likely-sounding of which were, 'Here make hillock' and 'hear, mark, listen'. It was all hopelessly tenuous, I thought gloomily. For a heady moment, I thought I'd cracked it; the metre of the syllables of the three words matched perfectly the names of the places I was bound for — 'Ayr — Lanark — Glasgow'. But this theory came unstuck over the initial letter of the second word; this was an 'm' — of that I was quite certain. It was tantalising, maddening, to know that but for a communications blockage concerning a few letters, I would now know the whereabouts of the Porcupine's lair. Something niggled at the back of my mind, an echo of a word or phrase that seemed to hold a clue to one of the words. But the more I tried to grasp it, the more elusive the memory became, and finally I gave up.

Early in the afternoon, we arrived at Bavelaw Castle near the hamlet of Balerno, on the northern slopes of the Pentlands — seat of the Braid family. Wattie presented a letter of introduction from Uncle Andrew to the major-domo, and we were made welcome. The Braids being away at one of their other estates, we had the run of the place (and the cellar) to ourselves.

As the great folk were absent, we dined frugally on beef and mutton with side-dishes of chicken, rabbit and pigeon. But the page was assiduous in recharging our goblets. We prevailed on him eventually to leave us, with two flagons of madeira to hand on the sideboard. If there's anything more pleasant than getting drunk with a congenial friend, I don't know what it is, unless it's getting drunk with a congenial mistress. Airily, we proceeded to set the world's problems to rights. Henry, Francis, Charles, Luther and the Pope ought to get together at a Summit Meeting and negotiate a settlement agreeable to all parties. Henry could give back Boulogne, if Francis would agree to keep out of Scotland. That would be okay by Scotland provided Henry called a halt to the Rough Wooing; that was an unfortunate misunderstanding anyway — the Scots would probably come round to accepting the marriage in the long run. If Luther was prepared to pay lip-service to Papal authority, then surely the Vatican could give a little on Jusification by Faith. All these matters could be settled with a bit of good sense and compromise. (At least that's how it seemed half-way through the second flagon.)

We were interrupted at length by a good-looking maid, who arrived to conduct us to our bedroom. As we weaved up stairs and along corridors, I could see by the way she took Wattie's arm and steered him round corners, that she fancied him. As she turned down our coverlet, I announced with ponderous diplomacy, "'shcuse me — think I'll get shome fresh air." Winking owlishly at Wattie, I stumbled back along the corridor, nobly prepared to sacrifice a night's sleep on the altar of friendship. It was a wasted gesture; scarcely ten minutes had passed, before the maid came flouncing down the passage.

"Bluidy sheep in wolf's claes," she snapped at me. "Yon pal o yeirs is a poofter, Ah'm thinkin."

"You mustn't rush him," I extemporized. "He's a bit shy, that's all." (That was a barefaced fabrication, but 'noblesse oblige'.)

"Huh! It's no shyness is the maitter wi yon yin," she retorted, and added nastily before storming off downstairs, "Ye'd best no keep him waitin."

I admit that I felt a slight trepidation as I slid between the sheets beside Wattie. Was he really bent, as the girl implied? Surreptitiously, I wriggled to the edge of the bed. But I needn't have worried. Feigning sleep (to avoid embarrassing explanations, I suppose), Wattie showed as little interest in me, as he had presumably, in the maid.

I woke with a parched mouth and pounding head, to find myself alone in the bed. Light was streaming through ancient arrow-slit windows. Checking my 'Nuremburg Egg' before rewinding it, I saw that it was five o'clock. Downstairs, I couldn't face food, and as Wattie and Tam were ready, we were soon on our way.

The fresh upland air began to exorcize the demons pounding away inside my skull, and I soon felt restored enough to twit Wattie about his misadventure the previous night. "Wasn't she to your liking?" I asked innocently. "I prefer blondes myself, but I wouldn't have turned down a juicy piece like that. Or was she the one that got away?"

A tide of crimson swept up Wattie's face. "Jist shu' up, will ye," he snarled, and urged his horse forward to be on his own, leaving me chuckling.

As we continued to ride south-westwards, the character of the land changed from the dramatic peaks of the previous day, to rolling moorland. The air was losing its keenness, becoming humid and heavy; meanwhile thunderheads were massing to the south.

"We'se be gey drookit, gin we dinna mak Linton or nin," commented Tam drily, glancing at the horizon.

Would I ever get the hang of this barbarous tongue? I wondered, as I tried to translate Tam's remark to myself; eventually, I decided that he meant we would get soaked unless we reached Linton before noon.

Linton! With the force and swiftness of a thunderclap, revelation burst upon me. I suddenly *knew*, with total certainty, what the first and third words that David Baxter had tried to tell me, were. They

85

were 'Hailes' and 'Linton'. On paper, the sounds which he had uttered could have been any of a vast number of alternatives. It was *hearing* the words spoken by another that had provided the key to their unlocking. Yesterday, Wattie had mentioned the name of our first stopping-place — 'Hailes'. That had started bells ringing in my brain; with Tam's uttering of the word 'Linton', the lock had clicked open.

A word, spoken aloud, has minute subtleties of inflexion and tone that distinguish it from others whose sound may at first seem identical. I don't believe that homonyms exist, strictly. Would anyone, hearing someone say, "We rode to London", think that he had said, "We rowed to London?" I would take my stand against all comers that he would not. Again, if anyone calls your name, even at a distance and in the midst of a noisy crowd, you tend to hear it, even though a score of similar sounds may be being uttered at the same time.

I couldn't remember any signs of industry at Hailes, though it was the sort of place which might have had mills in the vicinity; but of course I hadn't been looking for anything like that, then. Perhaps there might be something at Linton.

Containing my excitement, I caught up with Wattie, and by dint of 'speiring' about the ancestry of our absent hosts, the Braids of Bavelaw, restored him to good humour.

Skirting the forbidding Kitchen Moss, we came to an ancient trackway which would take us across the Pentlands to Linton, and whose approach was guarded by a grim and lonely hold.

"Cairns Castle," said Wattie, and spat on the ground. "Built a hunner yeir lang syne by Sir William Crichton that wis Chancellor, an whae had the Douglases kilt at the Black Dinner in Embro Castle. A gey ill lot they Crichtons."

Swinging south along the track, we climbed through rough and broken country towards a pass between two hills.

"Cauldstaneslap," said Wattie, when I asked what the pass was.

"Haud on sirs," cautioned Tam. "Ah dinna like the look o yon place. A bonny bit fur an ambush, gin ye ask me."

"Aye — but we're no askin ye, ye donnered auld runt," declared Wattie with affectionate rudeness. "This isna the Borders, man.

Nae reivers in these pairts. Gif we gang roond the lang wye by Wolf Craigs, we'll get drookit fur sure."

Grumbling, Tam subsided and we pushed on. As the land rose, the air, instead of getting cooler seemed to become steadily more oppressive. The sky grew darker by the minute, and thunder rumbled in the distance, causing our mounts to become restive. I dashed sweat from my forehead.

"How far to Linton?" I asked Wattie.

"Sax mile fae the heid o the pass. We'll be lucky tae mak it or yon lot breaks." And he gestured at the lowering cloudbanks.

"What sort of place is Linton?" I asked.

"Och, jist a pickle hooses an a kirk."

"No industry, mining — that sort of thing?"

Wattie swung round in the saddle and stared at me. "Will ye listen tae him? Industry? Minin? Ye've got tae be jokin. Man, there's nocht at Linton forbye sheep and peewees. The only minin's the gowd the Wee Folk are said tae howk fae the hills. Onywye, why a the interest?"

"Just asking," I said casually. "Must be confusing it with someplace else."

"Speak Scots," Wattie reprimanded me sharply. "Ye sud hae said, 'Jist speirin. Ah maun hae bin thinkin on anither bit.' Yeir accent's fine. Ye'd pass fur a Scot whae's lived in England, nae bother. But ye're supposed tae be a packman fae the Borders, mind. Try tae use a pickle mair Scots words in yeir crack." Wattie shrugged. "Still, it's no ma job tae learn ye, ony mair."

That was true. Wattie's brief had ended the day we left Hampton Court. He had never asked me the reasons for his coaching of me. Did he suspect that I was a spy? I wasn't too worried on that score; in a Borderer's scale of priorities, duty to one's country comes a long way below loyalty to a friend.

The slope steepened as we neared the height of land. "Ye maun pit a stoot hert tae a stae brae," I called to Wattie, quoting a Scots saw.

Wattie nodded approval. "Thon's be'er."

The jaws of the pass closed in on either side. A long tattoo of thunder rolled across a sky the colour of lead. At the top, we halted to breathe the horses. Before us, a wide shallow glen wound away southward through moorland plateau.

"Hist!" said Tam cocking his head.

Wattie sneered, "Whit's the maitter, ye daft — "; then continued in a changed voice, "In the name o the wee man — will ye get a load o yon!"

From the slopes all round us, a multitude appeared, as though conjured from the earth. From peat hags, clumps of heather and behind boulders they materialized, both men and women, to the number of perhaps a hundred. They were the strangest people I had ever set eyes on — dark-complexioned, black-haired, clad in a weird assortment of brightly-coloured (though worn and soiled) garments. Some of the older women were veiled like Moors and many, even some of the men, sported barbaric jewellery — pendants, brooches and earrings of heavy silver.

Assess, plan, act. 'Masterly inactivity,' prompted an inner voice.

In the few seconds that we had been staring at these apparitions, they seemed to have flowed over the terrain, encircling us completely. Steel rasped as Wattie and Tam drew their blades. I drew the wheel-lock from my satchel and wound up the spring.

One of their number, a tall commanding-looking man with curling moustaches, strode towards us and halted some yards off.

"Lay doon yeir wapens gif ye please," he said, with a kind of grave courtesy. He spoke a good enough Scots but with a foreign ring to it. "Ye'll nane o yese get hurt, gin ye dinna — "

"Haud yeir wheesht, ye low-born scoonrel," interrupted Wattie. "Dae ye daur speak tae a Ker like thon?"

I groaned inwardly. There's a time and place for heroics no doubt, but now was definitely not one of them. Tam evidently thought so too, for he whispered savagely, "Ca canny, Maister Walter. Are ye clean daft?"

But Wattie was past reasoning with. Raising his sword-arm he kneed his horse towards the man.

From somewhere in the crowd, a stone whirred through the air and struck Wattie on the temple with a meaty 'thunk'. Wattie sighed and slid from the saddle onto the heather.

"Drop thon pop-gun," snapped Tam from the corner of his

mouth, at the same time letting fall his sword.

Rage had swept over me at seeing Wattie hit, but the authority in Tam's voice cut through the red mist clouding my brain, and jerked me back to sanity. I dropped the wheel-lock.

The man picked up the weapons, then politely told us to dismount and strip. There was nothing for it but to comply, and presently we were standing in our shirts and hosen, which we were graciously allowed to retain. I prayed we wouldn't be subjected to a body search, when of course my precious money-belt would be discovered.

The two women who had been stripping the unconscious Wattie, suddenly left off what they were doing. They began laughing and calling out something that sounded like, "Bé...bé."

Like ripples from a stone dropped into a pool, the laughter spread throughout the assembly till they all seemed to be falling about. My initial fear that we had fallen into the terrible clutches of a band of sturdy beggars, was fast abating. Although wild-looking and rapacious, the manner of these people didn't seem particularly hostile, and their laughter was wholesome rather than threatening. Wattie's boots and top garments, which had been removed, were dropped beside him as though they had suddenly become taboo.

When the merriment had subsided a bit, one fellow who had been rifling through my satchel, approached the spokesman waving my testimonial from the Privy Council. It must have been the important-looking red seals that had attracted him; I doubted if he could read. The spokesman studied the document, then gave me a keen look.

"It seems they think ye're a braw leech," he said dubiously. "Ye look gey young tae me. Can ye cure the megrims?"

"I can try," I replied judiciously, sensing that here was an opportunity, which I had no choice but to grasp.

"Do ye say so?" He rattled off something to those about him in an incomprehensible dialect larded with a few Scots words. Then he turned again to me and said, "If ye wad be sae kind as tae accompany us." (As if I had a choice!)

My clothes and satchel were returned to me. When I was dressed, I turned to Tam, who had been stoically ignoring the curious stares which his lack of a nose provoked. "Well, this looks like the parting o the ways, Tam. I hope Wattie's no badly hurt. Still, I'm leaving him in good hands, and ye're no too far from help."

"Och, dinna ye fash yeirsel on oor accoont, Maister John," replied Tam, adding surprisingly, in good French, "C'est la vie. A pickle dunt on the heid — Masiter Walter'll be nane the waur. As fur yeirsel — jist ca canny an ye've nocht tae worry aboot. Thae folks is tinkler gypsies — theivin skellums, but no veecious, ken, gin ye dinna provoke them. An thon may no be sae easy, mind. Seemingly, they're expectin yese'll cure yin o them. Man ye'd be'er be guid — whit thae chiels dinna ken aboot cures is no worth kennin. They maun be fair desperate fur tae be askin help fae a 'gorgio'. Well, au revoir, et bonne chance, mon gar."

I shook his outstretched hand. "Bye Tam. Gie Wattie my regards when he comes to."

I set off with the gypsies on foot (my horse being commandeered), my mind in a whirl. My chief emotions were regret at the sudden parting from Wattie, frustration at my quest being interrupted just at this juncture, when the trail seemed to be getting warm, and anxiety as to the consequences of failing to live up to the gypsies' expectations concerning my medical skill.

THE QUEEN OF LITTLE EGYPT

MY SECRET HOPES that Tam and Wattie would summon help and eventually come to my rescue, were literally washed away. Minutes after parting from them, the storm burst in a ferocious downpour. The rain blotted out everything in sight, so that we seemed to be encapsulated within a screen of steel bodkins. Any trail that the gypsies might leave, would be utterly obliterated, I realized.

Within seconds, I was as sodden, chilled and miserable as it is possible to be, and, I am ashamed to admit, in mortal terror of being struck by the lightning bolts which flickered across the sky in rapid succession. The gypsies seemed indifferent to the weather, and pressed on at a punishing pace, in an easterly direction as far as I could guess.

For two hours by my reckoning (I couldn't be more accurate, because they had of course removed my Nuremburg Egg from my tunic), we pushed on over undulating moor and bogland, eventually descending a steep burnside to a narrow glen where their encampment was. Here were the elderly, the younger children, the nursing mothers and the horse-herd.

The leader conducted me to a roughly-made tent with a screen in front, behind which a fire blazed. I was told to enter. Inside was a harsh-faced woman and a boy of about twelve. No introductions were made, but I was given a change of clothes, and when I had rubbed myself dry and changed (the woman not bothered a whit while I did so), I was handed a bowl of delicious-smelling stew from a pot that bubbled over the fire. The lad was sent off and returned with my pedlar's pack containing my salves and Chineses needles.

The man waited in polite silence until I had eaten my fill, then handed me a cloak against the rain. "Gin ye're ready sir, we'll awa tae the Hoolet's Yett."

The Hoolet's Yett (Owl's Gate, in English) turned out to be a stone-built chapel some way down the burn, away from the main encampment. Inside, the light of many candles revealed a scene of barbaric comfort — brightly-coloured hangings and rugs, and a great couch of bracken and heather covered by soft deerskins. On this lay an enormous woman of about thirty. If she had been of normal stature, she would have been grossly overweight; but her tallness gave her a nobility of proportion that put me in mind of a recumbent Pallas Athene. Her skin was the colour of pale ivory, in contrast to the nut-brown of the other gypsy women. The face below the masses of raven-black hair was comely, but drawn with pain.

The man spoke to her deferentially in their own tongue, then turned to me. "She's sair troubled wi the megrim," he confided. "We've tried a wur skill, including a potion made fae henbane, which Ah've niver kenned fail afore; but tae nae purpose. Gin ye can dae onythin, we'll be fell indebtit tae yese."

"I'll see what I can do," I said, my voice sounding absurdly assured in my own ears, while within, my confidence shrivelled up.

The man retired, leaving me alone with the gypsy woman. "Where exactly does it hurt?" I enquired, feeling a total fraud.

She touched the side of her head behind the right eye. "There. when the attack comes, Ah feel seeck an Ah canna see richt. Ah see stars in ma heid forbye."

"How long have you been having these migraine attacks?"

"Och, Ah've aye had them. No that often ken, when Ah wis a bit lassie. But this last year they've been fair awfy. Every twa-three days jist lately. An they seem tae last mair langer ilka time."

"You're suffering at present?"

"Aye. Yin stertit this forenin. Ma heid wis fair spli'in. Ah can jist aboot thole it the noo." She smiled bravely at me, and I saw a gleam of hope in her eye.

Poor cow, I thought savagely — if only she knew! I looked out the case of golden needles and consulted the meridian chart which went with it. Migraine — that would be Point 20 on the Gall Bladder Meridian, located at the base of the skull behind each ear. Alternatively — Point 8 on the Liver Meridian behind the knee.

I asked her to sit up and push her hair out of the way. Then I selected a needle and tested it on the ball of my thumb for sharpness. Trying to control the shaking of my hand, I pushed the needle into the creamy skin, at what I hoped was Gall Bladder 20. She winced slightly but said nothing.

"That feel any better?"

"No — jist the same."

An hour later, I was still trying to locate Gall Bladder 20. My hands were slippery with sweat and my heart was thumping. The tension in the chapel was palpable, manifesting itself in my sticky palms and her rigid neck muscles. I was terrified in case the strain would trigger off another migraine attack. And of course that is just what happened.

Without warning, she gave a sharp cry and clapped her hands to her head. Agonized groans burst from her lips. Cursing, I got her to lie down and raise her dress above the knee. Liver 8 . . . I inserted the needle.

At the fifth attempt, the groans miraculously ceased. The woman's tense and quivering muscles relaxed.

"The pain — it's stoppit," she whispered.

I sagged with relief and amazement. It worked! Those Chinese needles actually worked!

Apprehensively, we 'counted ten' as it were, waiting for the pain to come crashing back. When five minutes had crawled past and all was still well, I carefully marked the spot behind her knee with a dab of kohl from a tray of cosmetics, after withdrawing the needle.

"Ye've cured me," said the gypsy in a wondering voice, her glowing eyes looking me full in the face. "Ye've done whit ma ain folk — the best leeches in the warld, couldna dae."

We looked into each other's eyes in a sort of triumphant daze. Warmth and empathy flowed between us. And something else. With the quick intuition and directness of her kind, she was a move ahead even of me (which is saying something). Her arms stretched out, her eyes closed, her lips parted. Next moment, we were wrestling in a passionate clinch.

Embracing this vast, yet splendidly-proportioned Amazon was a wildly exciting experience. She was quite uninhibited, returning my kisses with a gusto equal to, if not greater than, my own.

Gasping, we finally released each other. My heart thumped violently as she began to take off her clothes. I followed suit and within seconds we stood naked before each other. My senses swam at the sight of her magnificent body with skin like polished porphyry and proud breasts, whose nipples were already swelling to turgid cones. She lay back on the couch; her legs opened, disclosing her moist vulva beneath the jet-black Mount of Venus.

"Ye maun kneel afore a Queen," she whispered huskily. "The Queen o Little Egypt."

I obeyed. Her fingers twined themselves in my hair and drew my face between her thighs. My mouth fastened on that other mouth, my tongue found the swelling bud.

Her fingers tightened their grip, and she began to move rhythmically against me as my tongue busied itself with caresses. Moans and gasps burst from her throat, her movements quickened, became frantic. Then, with a broken cry, she came, in a long shuddering convulsion ...

We raised our heads and looked, smiling, into each other's eyes like successful conspirators, across the plain of her belly and the pass between her breasts.

"Come intae Egypt," she commanded softly.

Afterwards, luxuriously sated, we drifted off to sleep in each other's arms; her embrace was like snuggling into a vast feather bed.

I woke, to find only one candle still burning, and the Queen of Egypt snoring softly beside me. Remote chapels and love making seemed to be establishing a pattern in my life, I thought. Duty struggled with inclination, and after a sore battle, won. I slid stealthily from the couch and, retrieving my clothes, began to dress. But I had not been stealthy enough.

"Are ye tired o me a-ready?" she murmured reproachfully, sitting up on one elbow.

"It isn't that," I hastened to explain. "But I have to get back to Hailes, then push on to Linton. Urgent business. If it weren't," I assured her with a smile, "wild horses couldn't drag me away from my Queen."

"Och, ye're jist sayin thon," she said, but I could see that she was pleased. "But where's yeir hurry? Us Egyptians is fur Hailes an Linton. An we dinna tarry on the road. Ye'll mak be'er time wi us than on yeir ain."

94

"Oh well, in that case —," I said, pleased and relieved that duty and pleasure could be honourable bed-fellows. Then I had a blinding glimpse of the obvious.

"Wait a minute. Hailes is back towards Edinburgh. Linton's the other way."

She looked at me in puzzlement, then her brow cleared.

"It's no Linton in Peebleshire we're headin fur, nor Hailes by Embro whit some fowk's beginnin tae cry Colinton. We're fur Hailes an Linton in East Lothian. We've landit kinsfowk in thae pairts whit hae tane tae the gorgio life."

"What sort of places are they?" I asked with quickening interest.

"Hailes is a muckle castle the faur side o Haddington. Linton's a wee toon a mile or twa ayont Hailes."

"Any mining or industry?"

"No at Linton forbye the mills. But there's coal an iron warkins roon Tranent an at Gledsmuir — thon's the burgh muir o Haddington."

My pulse began to race. The East Lothian Hailes and Linton sounded definitely more promising than their western namesakes. Eastward Ho! with the gypsies then.

And so — despite being a 'gorgio' (non-gypsy), I became an honoured guest of the Egyptians. That I had cured their Queen (they weren't to know it was by luck rather than skill), plus the fact that she made no secret of our relationship, raised me virtually to the status of King of Little Egypt (well, King Consort, anyway). My horse and personal possessions (including my precious wheel-lock and Nuremburg Egg) were returned to me, and I 'moved in' — if the term can be applied to sharing a tent, with Barbara Faa, the Gypsy Queen.

The morning after my abduction, we struck camp and headed east, past St Catherine's Chapel by Glencorse Burn and so out of the Pentlands. We crossed the broad valley of the North Esk, passed Roslin with its castle and unfinished chapel and the great keep of the Borthwicks. All the gypsies were mounted, the men, (plus Barbara and myself) in front on ponies, the women behind on donkeys with the pack-animals.

95

We moved at a steady tripple that ate up the miles, so that by the afternoon we had climbed up out of the lowlands onto Fala Muir, where we pitched camp beside the hospice and church of the Holy Trinity at Soutra. Here the monks made us welcome, and in exchange for the gypsies' repairing utensils from the kitchens, replenished some of our supplies.

While we travelled, Barbara had told me something of herself and her people. The gypsies, she said, had come into Europe from the East, about a hundred and fifty years before, by way of Lower Egypt. One branch, consisting mainly of two tribes — the Faas and the Baillies, settled in Scotland where, under the late James V and his father James IV they were treated with favour and granted royal protection, with extraordinary privileges, until four years previously, when the relationship had suddenly turned sour. James V's favourite ploy was to mingle secretly with his subjects disguised as a wandering pedlar or gaberlunzie. He took up with the gypsies, who could then do no wrong in his eyes — until an enraged Romany thumped him with a bottle for trying to seduce his wife. Result — a Statute rushed through parliament, banishing the gypsies from Scotland on pain of death.

"Some o the Faas were feart an gaed awa doon tae Durham," said Barbara, "But the feck o us an the Baillies forbye bad in Scotland. We jist keepit wur heids doon. When Jamie passed awa, the Act becam a deid le'er."

Barbara's husband — John Faa, had, she claimed, been Earl of Egypt. (Whether the title was recognized by Faa clans other than her own, to say nothing of the Baillies, she didn't make clear.) When her husband was killed in a skirmish with the Baillies, Barbara succeeded to the throne as Queen — a position she would continue to occupy unless she married, when the Crown would pass to her husband.

"They wis fair queuein up tae coort me," she said, "But it wis the Croon they wis efter — the hale jing-bang o them, raither than masel. When Barbara Faa wads again, it'll be for luve — on baith sides." She gave me a heart-stopping look. "Hae ya a mind tae the Croon o Egypt, Jock?"

Though she said the words lightly, I knew she wasn't joking. I will admit that I was tempted, sorely tempted. To exchange the obscure and dangerous role of a spy, for the freedom of the gypsy life, marriage to a beautiful and passionate woman, and the Crown of Egypt thrown in as a bonus, seemed no bad bargain. But, though my heart was suddenly filled with a strange and powerful yearning, I heard myself make some flippant reply, and the moment passed for ever.

I have a quick ear for tongues, and by the time we had set up our tent at Soutra Aisle, I had picked up a few words of Minker Taval (Tinker Talk) — a mixture of Romany, Gaelic, cant and Shelta, this last an artificial 'secret' language from Ireland.

Remembering the scene at Cauldstaneslap, when the gypsy women had suddenly discontinued their stripping of Wattie, with cries of 'Bé', I asked Barbara what the word meant.

"Is this youse ettlin tae bu'er me up wi coampliments?" she said fondly. "'Bé' is whit the gorgios wad cry a 'bonny lass'."

I digested the implications of this, with mingled consternation and amusement. Was it possible that Wattie was a woman in disguise? — and if so, that I had been completely taken in over an extended period? With hindsight, I could think of some pointers — the comments of the Sir Bedivere's bosun and the maid at Bavelaw Castle. I tried to imagine him in a dress — with his good looks and slender build, he could certainly pass for a 'bonny lass'. But his deportment, his mannerisms, the way he wore his clothes — all were those of a virile young man. I tried to recall his speech for hints of a feminine intonation, but that line of thought ran into the sands. The Border inflexion tends to be high-pitched, with the sound rising at the ends of sentences, so that the differences between a man's and a woman's voice would not be nearly so obvious as they would say, in my own part of the world. I recalled that there had been authenticated cases of women disguising themselves as soldiers, accompanying their sweethearts to the wars.

Suppose for the sake of argument (for I found it almost impossible to accept) that Wattie *was* a woman — what sort of devious game was he playing? and was my own mission compromised in any way by our association? I kicked these questions around in my head, but was unable to come up with any

97

satisfactory answers.

On Barbara complaining of a slight recurrence of her migraine, I tried pressing Liver 8 with a finger instead of using the needle; to my delight, this worked immediately. I made sure that Barbara could locate the pressure-point exactly so that she would be able to treat herself, should she be troubled by migraine in the future.

Having heard that the gypsies were great fortune-tellers, I asked Barbara when we had eaten and retired to our tent, if she would read my palm. To my surprise, she seemed unwilling, but on being pressed reluctantly agreed.

She took my hand in hers, turned it over, and studied it for some seconds.

"I see blood," she said in a low voice. "Fire an steel forbye. The face o a fair-haired wumman — a bonny face." She looked at me searchingly, and I seemed to read reproach in her eyes. "It changes — changes; it isna bonny noo… " she dropped my hand with a shudder.

"What did you see?" I whispered, shocked despite myself. What had started as an innocent game, had suddenly turned bleak and ugly. The 'fair-haired woman' — could that be Jessie? And if so, did fate hold something terrible in store for her? (I discounted the possibility that Barbara might have invented her premonition out of jealousy).

"Ye shouldna hae asked me," she said, with a desperate note in her voice, and hurried from the tent.

Later, as we lay relaxed after love, with our arms round one another, I asked her again.

"Ah saw naethin, Jock. The face jist fadit awa."

It was a lie, but a lie kindly meant, and with that I had to be content. Perhaps it was for the best.

THE BATTLE FOR THE CROWN

THE FOLLOWING MORNING we pushed eastwards along the crest of the Lammermuirs, until our line of march intersected a broad track running north and south. We took the southern fork, which would lead us past Yester to Haddington. To our left swelled the rounded summit of Lammer Law. To our right, the land dropped steeply away to the valley of the Hopes Water.

Suddenly, Geleyr Matskalla, the moustachioed leader who had first brought me to Barbara, reined in, signalling to those behind him to halt. Wondering what had alarmed him, I quartered the landscape with my eyes, and strained my ears, but could pick up no untoward signals. Then, from behind the skyline of the Lammer Law appeared a frieze of figures armed with swords, bludgeons and the narrow poleaxes called Jedart staves. Geleyr and the other leaders galloped off shouting orders, and in an incredibly short time our band had dismounted and was forming into line of battle, with the able-bodied veterans in the centre, the younger men on the flanks, and the women and older children drawn up as a second line of defence behind the menfolk. Only the children below the age of fourteen and the mounts were removed from the scene, being escorted by those too old to fight towards a sheltered howe far down the hillside.

I felt the blood pound in my temples, as I tugged the wheel-lock from my satchel.

"No," said Barbara, laying a hand on my wrist. "Gypsies dinna fecht wi pooder. This is no yeir quarrel, Jock. Awa an tak chairge o the cuddies an the bairns. A guid man'll be sair needit gin we dinna best they blackgyairds — them's the Bailies come fur tae try conclusions wi the Faas at last, fur the Gypsy Croon."

"But I can't just leave you!" I protested wildly. "I must do something." The thought crossed my mind fleetingly, that Ascham would have a fit if he could see what I was getting myself into.

"Ye wad fecht fur Barbara?" she said softly, and the colour

flamed in her cheeks. "Oh Jock, Ah luve ye," and she hugged me to her. Next moment, she was composed and business-like.

She called to one of the teenagers running along the ranks with armfuls of weapons from the baggage train. I selected a sword similar to the one I had trained with under Martin at Hampton Court. To my amazement, Barbara armed herself with a long scythe-stick, then calmly proceeded to strip to the waist and kilt up her skirts.

"You're not going to fight, surely?" I said aghast, yet at the same time fascinated by the sight of that splendid naked torso.

"An why fur no?" she said matter-of-factly. "Look ahint ye."

I glanced back and saw the gypsy women clutching long knives, which they were obviously prepared to use.

By now, the Baillies were half-way down the slope separating our two forces. Although a total novice in this sort of situation, I could see that the Faas were in a desperate position. The Baillies, whose numbers roughly equalled ours, had chosen the site for their ambuscade skilfully. With the slope in their favour, if we failed to hold them in their first rush, their impetus would sweep us off the track, and down the steep slopes below, where inevitably we would be scattered and defeated.

To give us room to manoeuvre, our line advanced a little up the hillside, then halted, with weapons levelled to meet the Baillie charge.

As the gap between the forces dwindled, each began to shout its war-cry. For a few seconds screams and curses filled the air; then with a ring of steel, the two lines clashed together.

After that, I was aware only of my own immediate surroundings. A yelling bearded face loomed before me and a long dirk jabbed at my chest. Flinging up my sword, I partly deflected the weapon; the point struck me a glancing blow under the throat, turned on something and slid harmlessly below my armpit. Next moment, my attacker's rush carried him full tilt against me. I staggered and almost fell, then recovering, stepped back and slashed. Blood spurted from the man's arm and his dirk dropped. My blood was up now and I hurled myself into the press of fierce faces and flashing blades, hacking and thrusting like a man possessed. Perhaps the skills I had learned from Martin gave me some advantage, for when I came to myself I found I had cut my way clean through their line and was standing alone.

Gasping for breath, I turned and saw that the Faas had been pushed back almost to the edge of the path, and though fighting with grim determination, were continuing to give ground slowly. Except in the centre, where Barbara, her scythe-stick sweeping in great arcs, had cleared a space all round her. Her great size and obvious strength made her a fearsome opponent. Even as I looked, her whirling blade caught a Baillie full in the face, sending him reeling back with a hideous gash from brow to chin. Then my heart constricted as I saw that Barbara was sore wounded herself, her ribs showing white through ghastly cuts, as she moved. For a moment I stood stock-still in frozen horror, then a red rage possessed me, and yelling her name, I flung myself back into the battle. Heedless of cuts and stabs, I laid about me with a savage fury that may have daunted those who stood in my path, for in a few strokes I was beside her.

"Weel focht, Jock," she cried, and there was a fierce exhilaration in her voice. "The pair o us'll show them."

And we did. The circle around us slowly widened, became a breach — allowing Faas to surge through the gap and attack the Baillies in their rear. The Baillie advance faltered, halted, then slowly began to break up. The Baillie chiefs, realizing that the scales were tilting in our favour, suddenly called off their people.

In a twinkling, the Baillies were pouring away southwards with their wounded, and within minutes had vanished out of sight behind a fold of hillside, leaving the victorious Faas to lick their wounds. And terrible some of these wounds were — frightful gashes, so deep that bone and organs were plain to see. But my only thought was for Barbara; she made light of my concern however.

"Nocht that a pickle Adder's Tongue an St John's Wort willna mend," she said almost casually, though white with loss of blood.

Nevertheless, she let me staunch, salve and bind up her wounds, and generally fuss round her. The Faas limped a further mile downhill along the path, to a level stretch where we encamped. After pitching our tent and seeing that Barbara was comfortable, I took stock of my own condition. Beyond a deepish scratch in my thigh, and a few superficial flesh-wounds I seemed to be unscathed — for which I could probably thank Martin's rigorous training. When I undressed to examine my hurts more closely and tend them, I made an interesting discovery — the snapped-off point of a dirk embedded in the pewter Luckenbooth charm that I wore on a chain around my neck, and that was Jessie's parting gift. Soberly, I reflected that it may well have saved my life.

COMMUNION CLARET

NEXT MORNING, we 'hirpled' as the Scots expressively put it, down from the Lammermuirs, past the Hays' castle of Yester to the mighty keep of Lethington — the home of Sir Richard Maitland, and only a short distance from the Royal Burgh of Haddington.

Sir Richard was indebted to the Faas, Barbara explained. A few months earlier, using infusions of chicory, they had cured Sir Richard's brilliant young son William — a 'bejant' of St Andrews who had been sent home from the University, suffering from a bad attack of jaundice. As a result, the Faas had been invited to stay at Lethington whenever they should be in the vicinity.

We were greeted by Sir Richard's steward, given the freedom of the policies to camp in, and presently firewood, fresh meat, bandages and other supplies were sent out, so that the grounds soon resembled a field hospital. The gypsies were pressed to stay until their wounded were healed. I was astonished at how rapidly they began to recover from even the most frightful injuries; their life style makes them exceptionally strong and healthy I suppose, and their herbal remedies seem very effective.

For three days I lived with Barbara, tending her wounds or just lying beside her in the peace and privacy of our tent, talking and embracing. Or I would roll for her, cylinders of dried coltsfoot wrapped in thin paper from one of those small imported Bibles. She would put one between her lips and light it with a brand from our cooking-fire, draw in the smoke and puff it out — a captivating sight. Smoking the Bible! It seemed deliciously sinful. As I constructed one particular tube, the following passage from Daniel glared at me accusingly from the paper; 'He shall set at nought the GOD of their fathers; and shall be in the dalliances and desires of women ... ' It was a halcyon interlude, shot through with tenderness and passion. If she had repeated her offer, I think I would have accepted it. But she didn't, and on the fourth morning at Lethington, when she was well on the way to complete recovery, we both somehow knew that we had come to the parting of the ways.

She took a heavy gold ring from her hand and slipped it on my finger.

"Gin ye ever need help, show this tae a Faa, an they'll ken ye fur Jock Trummle whae cured their Queen."

We kissed — a fond tender kiss, then with a heavy heart I shouldered my pack and set off for Haddington.

As I walked past the Tower, an elegantly-dressed youth of about seventeen, strolled towards me peeling an apple.

"Leaving so soon?" he remarked, in a pleasantly cultured voice with only a hint of Scottish accent.

"I've nae cause to linger," I explained. "I only had a few scratches; anyway I'm no one o the gypsies."

"I see — just a fellow-traveller. You must be the chap with the golden needles. Father was hoping to have a chat with you. He can't resist any opportunity to add 'anither siller piece tae ma coffer o knowledge' as he puts it — all part of his Compleat Man act."

"What golden needles?" I asked innocently, wondering how this suave and self-possessed youngster had found this out; gypsies don't give much away to gorgios.

"Come off it," the other said, with a smile which robbed his words of any offence. "They don't call me Michael Wily — Michiavelli, at College, for nothing. When the Faas treated me for jaundice last time they were here, I practically became one of them. Naturally, I've heard about you on the grapevine."

So this was young William Maitland, no doubt on French leave this time, from St Andrews. I followed him into the keep and up a spiral staircase into the vast barrel-vaulted Great Hall, where a figure in a black furred gown was seated, scribbling at a table.

"I'll leave you with Father," said William Maitland, adding *sotto voce* before slipping away, "He'll probably read you some of his poems — you have been warned."

As Sir Richard did not seem to be aware of my presence, I approached the desk and cleared my throat. A pair of eyes blinked up at me myopically from behind thick-lensed spectacles.

104

"Losh man, Ah didna see ye. Ma een — they're gettin waur o the time. Weel, whit's yeir name an whit's yeir business."

"John Turnbull, Sir Richard. The golden needles used in healing; Yeir son said ye were interested."

"Thon smooth-tongued popinjay! Aye — so Ah am. So Ah am." Sir Richard got up. "Weel — let's be haein a keek at them, then."

I set down my pack and took out the case of needles. Sir Richard examined them with enormous interest and proceeded to grill me concerning their use.

"Perhaps ye could prick some sense intae the weemen o Haddington wi thae things," he said, shaking his head. "Fashion-conscious eediots. Aye wastin their siller on newfangled gear that's oot o date afore they can get it on their backs." He added hopefully, "Ah wrote a wee poem on the subject."

"Really Sir Richard? I don't suppose ye'd condescend to read it to a humble packman?"

"Och, Ah dinna see why fur no. Oor late King Jamie — him that wis cried the Gaberlunzie Man, an wham Ah had the honour tae serve personally, wisna above seekin the opinion o his common subjects." Taking a slim volume from a cupboard, he struck an attitude and began to read:

'Some wifies of the burgh toun sae wondrous vain are and
    wanton, they wot not what in the warld to wear.
On clathes they waste mony a croon, and all for
newfangledness
    of gear.
Sometimes they will bear up their goon, to shaw their
petticoat
    hingin doon,
And sometimes baith they will upbear, tae shaw their hose of
    black or broon; and all for newfangledness of gear.'

He looked up at me expectantly.

"Splendid, Sir Richard," I said, stifling a disgraceful urge to laugh. "Biting social commentary. On a par wi Sir David Lindsay's 'Three Estates', I'd say."

"Ye think sae?", he replied, obviously pleased and relieved. "Aye — Davie Lindsay's no sic a bad makar, no sae bad ava. Ah ken him

105

weel; he bides jist up the road at Garleton, the ither side o Haddington."

I endured an hour of Sir Richard reciting his doggerel, sandwiched between some rather good stuff by Robert Henryson, Gavin Douglas and William Dunbar, the last two also East Lothian men, Sir Richard informed me. At last I was dismissed with the gracious injunction to report to the major-domo who would "see yese is a richt."

I was waved through a doorway and found myself in the kitchen. Here I was served a plain meal of salmon followed by venison washed down with small beer. While I was eating, my ears picked up a sound above the clatter of pots and serving dishes — a rhythmic thumping noise which seemed to be coming from a remote part of the keep below me. Idly, I wondered what was causing it, then dismissed the speculation from my mind. On leaving, the major-domo gravely presented me with a purse and a parcel of cast-off clothes (to replace those which had suffered in the gypsy battle, I supposed).

As I stepped outside the great iron 'yett' (as the Scots call a gate) of the keep, I noticed a packhorse standing near the entrance. I had covered perhaps a quarter of the mile separating Lethington from Haddington, when I was overtaken by a man leading the same packhorse. We greeted each other perfunctorily and he slowly drew ahead. I had forgotten the incident, when I spotted a shiny object lying in the dust of the road. Picking it up, I examined it with growing curiosity. It was a brass tube between two and three inches long, closed at one end by a brass disc which was perforated in the middle. What its purpose was, I couldn't imagine; was it in some way connected with the rhythmic noise I had heard in Lethington Tower, and if so, had it dropped from one of the pack-horse's panniers? With a stirring of excitement, I dropped the thing into my satchel and hastened to overtake the man leading the packhorse — a hard job with my heavy backpack.

Topping a rise, I looked down on a river winding through haughs, and beyond it a vast cruciform church outside a walled town of considerable size — the Royal Burgh of Haddington. Even at a distance of several hundred yards, I could see that the church,

and many of the town's buildings were badly damaged —
presumably as a result of Hertford's Raid the previous year. There
was my packhorse and its master not fifty yards ahead of me.
Coming level, I greeted the man — a stocky fellow with a red open
face, and asked him if he could tell me the way to Linton. He looked
at me appraisingly for a moment or two, then replied cheerily, "Aye
— Ah'm gangin thon gait masel. We'll can traivel thegither. Thon
pack o yeirs looks an awfy wecht, man. Gie's it here an Ah'll fix it
tae the cuddy's load." And taking some straps from one of the
panniers, he secured my pack between the two.

We exchanged names and occupations — his was Alexander
Tait, servant to Sir Richard Maitland. As we came level with the
huge church on the far bank of the river, I commented on the
damage, now starkly obvious.

"English bastards!" Tait spat on the road. "It micht hae been
waur Ah suppose; they havena strippit the roof affa St Mary's —
yet. They promised tae dae that next time they come this wye."

Entering the suburb of Nungate, we had to battle through a huge
crowd streaming past us towards the bridge and St Mary's Church.
In their midst walked a tall cleric with a smug beaming face,
accompanied by a short, full-bearded, *forceful*-looking man,
bearing aloft a double-handed sword of inordinate length. An aura
of terrible, impressive fanaticism seemed to emanate from this
extraordinary pair, more than cancelling out anything comic about
their appearance.

Again Tait spat. "Geordie Wishart, the Protestant preacher, an
his self-styled protector John Knox. Pals o the bloody English on
accoont o the Reformation's takin ower doon there. Cardinal
Beaton's sworn tae burn thon Wishart gin he can catch him. An
mair power tae his elbow, says Ah." (This confirmed what Ascham
had told me at my briefing, concerning these two. At the time, I
thought what an extraordinary coincidence it was that I should encounter this pair of secret allies of the English. But it was not really so
surprising, as Haddingtion was the chief base for their activities, as I
was shortly to find out.)

As we travelled east along the main Dunbar road, I began to
develop my persona of Jock Trummle quacksalver, for Tait's

107

benefit — tentatively at first, then with growing confidence as Tait seemed to swallow all I was saying, without question. Presently, I felt secure enough to risk a direct question or two without arousing suspicion.

"Do ye often make this journey?" I asked conversationally.

"Oo Aye — everra twa-three weeks this past twalmonth."

"Carrying?"

"Ye've got me there, pal. The Maister disna pye me fur tae speir. 'Alex,' says he, 'thae pokes is a sealit an coontit; ye'll no meddle wi whit's in them, an ye'll no ask ony questions — a richt?' Oo, Ah wis black affrontit Ah can tell ye. 'Sir Richard,' says Ah, richt deegnified ken, but lettin him see Ah wis vexed like, 'there's nae ca fur tae tak thon line wi me, whae's served ye thae twenty year. They dinna cry me Honest Eck fur naethin.' Oo, he clum doon efter thon, Ah can tell ye. 'Alex,' says he, a gracious noo mind, 'thon's the verra reason Ah'm askin ye. Because Ah ken ye're tae be trustit.' Ach, it's a cushy number. Ah deliver ma pokes at the Abbey, in exchange fur some packages — no verra big but an awfy wecht mind. Thon's aye guid fur a gill an a crack. Oo, she's a richt randy piece thon Prioress, Ah can tell ye. No that Ecky Tait's had only luck wi her. Then it's on tae Hailes tae offload ma packages, an there's aye a bit drink siller there fur Honest Eck."

Hailes! I couldn't believe my luck. I had been angling for minnows and had landed a pike. I had the feeling that the pattern of Operation Porcupine — hazy and tenuous up till now, was on the verge of taking on definition.

"I thought ye said ye were going to Linton," I said, managing to sound casual, despite my racing heart.

"Hailes — Linton, it's the same bit; they yin's but a step fae the ither."

Soon after, we reached the Abbey bridge — a massive modern buttressed structure of three spans. We crossed the Tyne* to the nunnery buildings, most showing fire scars and signs of recent repair, obviously the legacy of Hertford's Raid. A handsome young nun conducted us down a corridor to an oak door, which she

* _Not to be confused with its Northumbrian namesake. (Transcriber)_

rapped on and opened, then announced us.

We were ushered into a comfortable chamber, hung with tapestries and with fresh rushes on the floor. Despite the season, a fire crackled in the grate. Seated at a writing-desk piled with correspondence, was a rosy-cheeked nun of maybe fifty. She surveyed us with mischievous blue eyes, then rose.

"Yeir messages is a ready fur yese, Alex," she said. "When ye get tae Hailes, ye can tell thon Patrick Hepburn Ah havena forgie-en him yet fur thon wee trick he plyed on me." She eyed me roguishly, then said to Alex, "Come on, introduce us tae yeir bonny freend."

"He's cried John Turnbull, Reverend Mother," said Alex. "A traivellin quacksalver."

"A quacksalver! An me wi a sair back. Is thon no a bit o luck? Nae doot ye'll be a bit drouthy Alex — as per usual. Sister Clare here'll tak ye tae the Guest Hoose whaur ye can sample wur latest brew. Ah'll send yeir freend alang when he's seen tae ma back."

Tait bowed and backed to the door. Sister Clare seemed reluctant to move. A flush crept above her wimple.

"An whit are youse hingin aboot fur, ye jealous bitch?" snapped the Prioress. "Awa wi ye instanter, or ye'll no be gettin atween ma bedsheets fur a gey lang time."

Tait fled, followed by a scarlet-faced Sister Clare.

The Prioress exploded into gales of laughter. Subsiding, she took a flagon and two chalices from a cupboard, and poured. "Communion claret," she said, handing me a brimming cup. "But it's no bad."

She took a deep swig, staring at me over the brim with a direct, hungry look that had only one meaning. For once, I was lost for words.

"Cat got yeir tongue, lad," she said softly. "Whit's the maitter? Dinna be shocked at whit Ah telt yon sonsy besom. Beggars canna be chosers; an yince ye get used tae it, a wumman's as guid in bed's a man. Be'er in some wyes fur she's gentler an'll tak mair pains fur tae satisfy ye. But fur a that, Ah whiles fancy a man — especially if he's young an bonny like yeirsel."

Flattery will get you everywhere, I thought, feeling the familiar stirring in my loins, as I helped this amazing woman to remove her habit. I had to admit she still had a good figure, and in her day must have been quite a looker. But hell — old enough to be my mother! Oh well, lie back and think of England, I told myself.

Which is pretty well what happened. Taking charge, she mounted me, skilfully timing the urgent thrusting of her hips to bring herself towards her orgasm, without precipitating mine. "Dinna come afore Ah'm ready," she gasped, "Or Ah'll kill yese." The sight of her moving body straddled above mine, with her breasts bouncing like jellies, her eyes slitted and lips parted in ecstasy, was unbearably erotic. How I held back I shall never know (probably sheer terror at the prospect of frustrating her), but somehow I managed, finally exploding inside her, as she climaxed in a series of rippling jerks.

"Oh, thon wis guid," she sighed contentedly, looking down at me with sweat trickling between her breasts. "Ye ken yeir job, Jock Trummle. Elizabeth Hepburn's no been pleesured like thon, syne Ah had Harry Cockburn atween ma legs — a proper man fur a that he's a freend tae thon traitor Wishart."

"We aim to please," I murmured, more amused than offended by this outrageous creature's candour. For some reason, this remark sent her off into screams of laughter. She was still wiping her eyes when demure in her habit once more, she showed me out of her room. (Sex and religious establishments again, I thought inconsequently.)

"Ye're welcome at St Mary's ony time Jock," she said at the door, giving me a smacking kiss. There was no illusion of anything like love between us. Each had given the other something they wanted, that was all. But we parted in warm friendship.

Before collecting Alex from the Guest House, I surreptitiously examined the panniers of his stabled pack-horse. As I had expected, one was frayed at a corner — enough for the passage of the brass cylinder I had picked up in the road. Undoing the lid, I peeked inside and saw a number of wooden boxes, tied and sealed — obviously the 'messages' which he had exchanged for the 'pokes'. Clearly, there was no possibility of my examining the contents.

We were speeded on our way by a frigidly polite Sister Clare. "Hey — did yese make it wi the Prioress?" asked Alex, in tones half

110

of envy, half of awe.

"Ye heard what the lady said, Alex. I was simply treating her back."

"Oh aye — pu the ither yin. They're an awfy lot thae Hepburns. Patrick Hepburn — Lord Hailes, Earl o Bothwell tae the likes o us yins, ken whit he did a wee while back? Lockit up thon Prioress in her ain Abbey! Arran himsel had tae send sodgers fur tae let her oot."

We followed the road along the south bank of the Tyne, past the estate of Stevenston, the worst scars of Hertford's devastation partly masked by the greening countryside. Further on, the landscape changed dramatically, from flat cornland to rugged whin-covered slopes dominated by the vast towering hump of Dunpender Law. The Tyne now entered a defile, changing from a placid stream to a rushing torrent. In this dark and narrow place we came to Hailes Castle looming on a crag above the river. We stopped for Alex to remove my pack from the horse.

"Hopeless site for a castle," I observed in surprise, as I shouldered my pack. "What on earth possessed them to build it down in this hole?"

"Ye'll soon find oot," said Alex with a rueful chuckle. "Sorry pal, Ah forgot tae warn ye. Ah'll try an see if Ah canna get yese aff."

A guard strolled out of the castle gatehouse, past the straggle of mean dwellings that comprised the castleton, and onto the road, blocking our passage.

"Hullo there Ecky. Whae's this wi ye?"

"A quacksalver Ah met up wi on the road. He disna ken aboot the toll. Och — jist let him by, man."

"Nae chance. The captain wad hae the hide affa me gin he fand oot."

I parted with some of the coins from the purse I'd been given at Lethington, and after bidding farewell to an apologetic Alex, was allowed to continue on my way. I walked along a steep bank above the Tyne, which I crossed after a mile by a sturdy stone bridge, to find myself in the little town of Linton.

I had formed no plans as to my next move, but clearly my priority must be to establish a base from which to plan and execute

111

'Operation Porcupine'.

First a 'pre-recce' as Ascham would have said. After quenching my thirst at an alehouse, where I was allowed to leave my pack, I strolled down the main street, and after a short gap, found myself in the separate townlet of Prestonhaugh where stood the parish kirk for both communities. Here, not far from a well dedicated to a St Baldred, a lade from the Tyne fed a water-mill, whose kiln had an extraordinary roof shaped like a jester's cap. Retracing my steps along the river bank, I discovered more mills below the bridge. Here the Tyne swirled dramatically through a narrow gorge before plunging into a linn — hence the name of the town, I supposed. I was beginning to form an impression of a strange secret little place — a double town lost in a hollow of the rolling landscape, full of the plash of falling water and the clacking of mill-wheels.

Back at the alehouse, feelers out for useful information, I chatted to the publican one Gibbie Cochrane. Gibbie was a friendly garrulous little man, clearly bent on making the most of an opportunity to impress a stranger to the locality, by holding forth about the background and amenities of the place.

"It's a graun wee place Linton," he declared. "The best fairms in Lothian, which is tae say in a Scotland, is roonaboot. We've a Curlin Club, foondit seivin year back. A feck o important fowk's been coneckit wi Linton. Ye'll hae heard tell o Gavin Douglas the makar, son tae Erchie Douglas that wis 'Bell the Cat'?"

" 'Of this nation I knew also anon,
Great Kennedy and Dunbar yet undeid ...',"
I was able to quote, having had some of his verses recited at me that morning. "That chap?"

"Ah 'specs ye're richt," replied the publican, obviously impressed. "Ah'm no really intae the Poetry masel, ken. Weel Gavin Douglas wis pastor o Linton an rector o Haugh back in Jamie the Fowert's time." And Gibbie went on to catalogue the celebrities associated with the area, from King Loth and St Baldred in the misty past, to William Wallace, Harry Hotspur, and John Mair the famous historian.

"Ye'll be saying next the Pope's been here," I said with a grin.

"Weel — ye'd no be faur wrang at that," replied Gibbie, quite

112

seriously.

"Go on!"

"Thon's no a word o a lee. A hunner year back, Aeneas Sylvius Piccolo — somethin-or-ither, Ah canna jist get ma tongue roon thae Eytie names, onywye him that becam Pope Pius II, wis shipwrecked at Dunbar. He walked in his bare feet — in winter mind, tae gie thanks fur his deliverance, a the wye tae Whitekirk. Thon's jist up the road a wee. The fowks o Linton happit the puir body in blankets an steepit his feet in het wa'er. But it didna dae muckle guid seemingly, fur he had the rheumaticks a his days efter." And Gibbie shook his head over the vagaries of foreign clergy.

I asked Gibbie where I could find a bed for the night.

"Och — ye've no faur tae seek. Gae doon the street an past the Preston turn-aff. Then tak the road tae yeir left an ye'll come tae Markle. The monks'll pit yese up, nae bother.

"Yon bit wis the birthplace o modren Scotland, ye could say," continued Gibbie, launching into his compulsive patter once more. "Hit wis at Markle ken, that the Picts an the Scots furst jined up thegither as the yae nation, fur tae gie Athelstan an his ermy o Northumbria a richt hammerin. There wis this muckle cross appeared in the sky ken, like the yin St Andraw wis...'

But I was no longer listening, for the name 'Markle' seemed to have started a chain of echoes sounding in my head. Then suddenly it clicked. 'Markle' — that was the second of the three words that David Baxter had tried to tell me! I felt like doing a cartwheel in the middle of the pub. Hailes, Markle, Linton — together they would furnish me with the clues I needed to track down the Porcupine.

SERPENT IN EDEN

MARKLE TURNED OUT to be quite an extensive little community — a township comprising secular as well as monastic buildings, with a chapel dedicated to — wait for it, St Mary. The Porter summoned the Guest Master, who showed me into the Guest House by the main gate; the only other guests were a grain-chandler from the Merse and a Leith merchant. It was all very neat and plain — clean straw on the floor, beds with clean sheets, pillows and mattresses, clean towels, unchipped crockery and scoured pewter. We were served a horrible meal of boiled fish and pease porridge washed down with acidic beer. (I suppose I should have been more grateful, as the number of monastic establishments that still bothered to cater for guests, was fast dwindling.)

With the Vespers' chanting sounding in my ears (vividly evoking memories of Ely), I went off for a solitary walk in order to think out the next stage of my campaign. Leaving the monastery precincts, I encountered a singular-looking pair, thick in talk beside the gatehouse. One was a great burly fellow in stained riding leathers, the other gaunt and bearded, clad in a parson's cassock. As I passed them, the burly one clapped the priest on the shoulder, and they both guffawed at some private joke.

It was a delightful place to stroll and meditate. To the east I could glimpse the North Sea, to the North loomed the arresting cone of North Berwick Law, with beyond it the Firth of Forth and the suggestive twin bumps of the Lomond Hills in Fife, while to the south, the Lammermuirs rolled along the horizon. Below the ridge on which the main buildings stood, two miniature lochs gleamed in the afternoon sunlight.

I weighed up the facts in my possession. Hailes, Linton and Markle, seen from a bird's eye view, would form the apexes of an equilateral triangle, and this area contained the secret of the Porcupine; this was the theory I must work on unless new evidence proved otherwise. Sir Richard Maitland of Lethington and the nuns of St Mary's Abbey were probably involved in the business up to the hilt. So far, the only bit of physical evidence I possessed, was the curious brass cylinder I had found on the road between Lethington and Haddington, which I was sure had dropped from the load carried by Alex's packhorse. Taking it from my satchel, I examined it again; this time, I noticed that the disc sealing one end, was slightly wider in diameter than the tube itself, thus creating a projecting rim at that end.

What on earth could the tube be? Alex delivered a light load at the Abbey, and picked up a number of heavy packages in exchange. Assuming that what he offloaded at the Abbey was a consignment of the brass tubes, it seemed logical to suppose that the packages contained the previous load of brass tubes which had been filled with something in the interim. Filled with what? A mental picture of the iron cartridge case containing the charge for the carbine I had practised with at Hampton Court, flashed into my brain; it was tempting to assume that the brass tubes must also be cartridge cases, designed to contain a charge of either powder or powder and ball. Assuming for the sake of argument that this was so, there were two important differences between the iron and the brass cases. The iron cases — about a dozen all told, were not expendable, and eventually all had to be recharged, whereas the brass cases would seem to be being produced on a scale suggesting that they must be expendable. The expense and labour involved in producing such numbers, could surely only be justified if the Porcupine were indeed a rapid-fire weapon as Ascham had postulated, when re-charging expended cartridge cases would be out of the question. The other difference was that the iron cartridge cases were perforated at the side, to allow the charge to be ignited through the touch-hole; the brass case was perforated at the *rear*. I couldn't imagine how this would apply to any known system of ignition. All of these were variants of a basic principle; sparks or flame ignited powder in a pan, which in turn ignited the powder-charge in the barrel via a touch-hole.

Putting such technical matters aside for the moment, I considered the localities, trying to assess their suitability as sites for the manufacture of the Porcupine. According to Barbara, the basic

115

raw materials — iron and coal, were worked in the vicinity of Tranent and Haddington. Coal would be used for forging the iron, once the ore had been smelted with charcoal prepared from local timber. Or, if imported iron were being used, Aberlady — the Port of Haddington was sited conveniently close. The shaping of the metal into the complex and intricate parts of which a weapon such as the Porcupine must surely be made up, would call for skills and facilities immeasurably greater than those obtaining in a local blacksmith's forge. Also the manufacture would have to be done in secret. Where could such skills and facilities be deployed secretly? The answer fairly shouted itself in my head — castles, monasteries, mills; in other words, Hailes, Markle, Linton. Throw in Lethington Tower and St Mary's Abbey for good measure, and you had the clincher.

Tremendously excited now, and sure that I was on the right track, I skirted the larger of the two lochs and struck south across pastureland towards Pencraik — an extensive hill lying just outside the triangle and close to its southern apex. At the summit, an arresting prospect unrolled itself below me. Away to the east, a town and castle which could only be Dunbar, perched beside the sea. To the north, the great tower of Whitekirk rose above rich fields of corn and pasture, with beyond it the Bass thrusting up out of the sea. Westwards, I could see the strange Garleton Hills, St Mary's Abbey, and beyond, the tower of St Mary's Church and the walls of Haddington. Before me, to the south across the valley of the Tyne, loomed the tremendous bulk of Dunpender Law, and below it the stark mass of Hailes Castle crouching darkly in its gorge beside the river.

The whole scene was bathed in golden sunlight — a dramatic lovely landscape, peopled past and present by saints, scholars, poets, preachers, statesmen, pilgrims and warriors. Here was Eden — but Eden with its hidden serpent. For behind this smiling richness lurked something ugly and evil which unless scotched would spawn destruction on a hideous scale. In sober mood, I descended the track that led down Pencraik to Linton, passing an ancient standing stone that I thought must be the 'Loth Stone' that Gibbie Cochrane had said marked the grave of that king.

116

As I walked, the whole Porcupine project impressed me more and more by its simplicity, boldness and cunning. Just as you wouldn't expect a thief to come in by the front door, the last place anyone would expect the Scots to manufacture their secret weapon, would be right in the middle of the main invasion route from England. Who would suspect monasteries and castles of harbouring arms factories? Yet the factors essential for the successful production of the weapon were all here — castles and monasteries with their disciplined communities, providing strong, commodious buildings where manufacturing plant could be installed and operate in secrecy; mills, whose machinery might be adapted to the production of gunpowder or components. Another thought — a monastery or nunnery would be an ideal source for the large amounts of urine needed for the corning process, which the production of modern gunpowder entailed. Raw materials, land and sea communications, an abundant food supply, populous burghs to supply commodities and trained artisans — the whole infrastructure necessary for the Porcupine's creation was there. The very dispersal and lack of centralization in such a scenario constituted one of its strengths. Machinery and components could be easily dismantled and hidden away if prying eyes came too close — as must have been the case when Hertford rampaged through the area the previous year. A picture formed itself in my mind — a vast network of intelligence, forged by keen, hostile minds, and enmeshing the countryside in a web of menace.

Diffuse though its organization might be, the Porcupine project must surely be masterminded by a single individual. My task was clear; from this moment on, my spying could begin in earnest, dedicated to tracking down the lair of the Porcupine itself, and uncovering the identity of its Keeper.

THE LAD WI THE GOWDEN PREENS

IN THE COURSE of the next fortnight, I circumnavigated the area I had viewed from Pencraik Hill. In my role of quacksalver, I called at farms, hamlets, family seats, and the four burghs of Tranent, Haddington, Dunbar and North Berwick. By means of bearings taken with my compass, distances recorded on milestones or computed with the aid of my Nuremburg Egg, and topographical details learned in conversation, I was able to construct a map, which I found enormously useful for reference purposes.

The fact that I was generally well-received, owed at least as much to the ready flow of patter which I soon developed, reinforced by the Privy Council's testimonial, as to any actual cures which I was able to effect. I avoided more ambitious treatments such as 'to cut for the stane' which though technically covered by my licence, were quite outside my competence. My salves and poultices, combined with the patient's own belief in their efficacy, may on balance have been slightly beneficial. At least in all likelihood they weren't actively harmful. My golden needles, I kept firmly hidden away in their case. They'd worked in Barbara's case, but I wasn't going to press my luck.

I soon discovered that as a member of the medical fraternity (though on the very bottom rung of that particular ladder), I was treated more as a friend than as a stranger, and that people tended to speak freely and unguardedly in my presence. So, by dint of unobtrusive 'speiring', and keeping my eyes and ears open, I was able gradually to build up a considerable store of information. An unsuspecting outsider would have learned nothing; I knew what I was looking for, and that made all the difference. A dropped word here, a casual reference there, a string of packhorses spotted at a time and a place no packhorse would normally be found, men on foot or horseback posting around the countryside with somewhat greater frequency than might be considered normal, an air of preoccupation among some of the households where I was given a bed for the night, lights and the clack of machinery coming from a mill, long after most good folk were asleep — all these fragmentary clues gradually accumulated, consolidating into a pattern of evidence, which confirmed and amplified my original hypothesis. I tabulated my findings in my head as follows:

*The Theatre:** The area in which Porcupine-related activity seemed to be concentrated, formed an oval whose long axis stretched from Haddington eastwards to the mouth of the Tyne, and whose short axis extended from Whitekirk in the north to Dunpender in the south. This area comprised the valleys of the Peffer and the lower Tyne — a sort of double strath, each part of which was separated from the other by a low ridge extending from Pencraik to the Garleton Hills. In the centre of this oval, was the Hailes-Markle-Linton triangle.

Separate from, and lying to the north and west of this oval, and connected to it by roads and tracks, were the Port of Haddington, i.e. Aberlady, the vast Hepburn stronghold of Luffness, the castleton and Palace of Seton — home of Lord Seton, and the coal and iron working area round Tranent. These places I thought of as 'outlying bases' or perhaps 'supply-centres' for the main area.

The image which formed itself in my mind, was of a great spider's web — first the outlying ring of 'supply-centres', then the inner one of the Tyne-Peffer oval, finally the central nub of the Hailes-Markle-Linton triangle. The radiating strands connecting these concentric rings, I imagined as the lines of communication and the system of Intelligence. The question as to who was the spider sitting in the middle of the web, leads on to the next heading.

The Protagonists: The dominant family of the area was the Hepburns, with seats at Luffness on the coast near Aberlady, Waughton Castle west of Whitekirk, and of course Hailes Castle, the stronghold of Patrick Hepburn, third Earl of Bothwell. He came high on my list of suspects for the masterminding of the Porcupine project, and seemed a colourful and unscrupulous

See Wainwright's Map. (Transcriber)
119

character. There was no difficulty in unearthing the salient facts about him; these nobles lived their lives in the full glare of public affairs and their doings were common gossip. Opinions about him among those whom I asked were mixed — fear (especially if the interrogee was a sympathiser of the Reformers), admiration, distrust, wary respect. All seemed to agree on one point however — Patrick Hepburn was a dangerous man to cross. I draw up a mental case-history of the man on the following lines:

Patrick Hepburn, 3rd Earl of Bothwell

Born 1512 only son of Adam 2nd Earl (killed at Flodden).

1528 Forgiven for giving treasonable help to Lord Home. Arrested for helping Border reivers.

1531 Allies with Earl of Northumberland because of 'wrongs by King of Scots'. Negotiates to become English subject.

1538 Removed from lordship of Liddesdale. Banished from Scotland. Lives in Venice.

1542 Returns to Scotland on death of James V.

1543 Threatens to get Regent Arran (weak, dithering) deposed for protecting Reformers — Wishart & Co. (Reformers generally suspected of favouring alliance with England.) As Sherriff of East Lothian and Cardinal Beaton's 'strong man', wages campaign against Wishart; cracks down on Haddingtonians attending Wishart's sermons in St Mary's, etc. Opposes Henry VIII's plan for match between infant Mary Queen of Scots and Prince Edward of England. (Henry's aim — ultimate unification of England and Scotland.) Champions dowager-queen Mary of Guise (widow of James V) against Arran who at first favours match. Divorces wife Agnes Sinclair in vain bid for hand of Mary of Guise (for political not romantic reasons).

1544 Aggressive stance against Hertford when latter invades Lothians (but backs down). Summonsed by Scots Parliament to account for earlier treasonable letter to Hertford, but let off.

1544 Steps up anti-Wishart campaign to scale of witch-hunt.

N.B. Described by Sadleyr (English envoy re marriage negotiations) as 'vain, insolent, full of folly'.

An intriguing catalogue! Could Hepburn be summed-up as a traitor-turned-patriot, displaying all the zeal of the converted? (Or was that too simplistic a view?) And if so, could last year's summons for treason be perhaps a deliberate blind on the part of the Scots authorities, to provide cover for Porcupine-related activities? the timing of the summons and his forgiveness, suggested a put-up job. (Perhaps his incarceration of Elizabeth Hepburn the Prioress, was also a blind, designed to allay any suspicion of collusion between the two of them.) Certainly, Hepburn appeared to be taking a clear-cut patriotic stance at present — supporting Beaton's pro-French, anti-Reformer, anti-English, strongly 'Nationalist' party, and taking a tough line with the plastic Arran when he wavered towards a pro-Reformer or pro-English policy.

Other Hepburns in the area who wanted watching were my hot-blooded Prioress Elizabeth (the Abbey I discovered owned the teind of the Gimmers Mills in Haddington, which might also be significant), and the family of Sir Patrick Hepburn of Waughton Castle. Sir Patrick, at whose castle I had stayed the night following my visit to Markle, had a son George Hepburn — a jovial boor with a shock of auburn hair. George had recently been parson of Prestonhaugh but had leased the office to his friend Nicol Crichton — a bony scarecrow with a great hooked nose and straggly beard, the presentation being made by — (surprise, surprise) the Earl of Bothwell. This odd couple whom I had already encountered at Markle, I had observed at Waughton entering the great circular doocot (Scots for dovecote).

Other 'Hostiles' on my list included the following: Sir Richard Maitland of Lethington (definite), Lord Seton (probable), and the Lindsays of Garleton (possible). Sir Richard and Lord Seton had all the correct background credentials for Freedom Fighters. Both (like Earl Bothwell) had had fathers killed at Flodden; together they had engineered the escape of Cardinal Beaton after his imprisonment by Arran; both had been personal friends of James

V, and were loyal supporters of the Stewart house.

Between the Garletons and Kilduff Hill is a lovely hidden valley, 'hanging' some two to three hundred feet above the Peffer levels. In this secluded place, I experienced a strange sense of other-worldliness. Ascham, whose knowledge of Greek had unlocked for him a world of pagan beauty shut to myself, had once spoken to me about something the Greeks called 'temenos' — a hidden sanctuary of the Gods. I had not really grasped what he had been driving at then; I did so now.

At the head of this valley, among the spurs and corries of the miniature range of the Garleton Hills, I tracked down the twin Lindsay seats — Garleton Castle and the Byres. In the former, I found the famous laird of Garleton — Sir David Lindsay of the Mount (the handle refers to a subsidiary property in Fife) in residence. Sir David had been Lord Lyon King of Arms to James V, but because of his anti-clerical sentiments, was out of favour with James's widow Mary of Guise, and consequently spent less and less time in the capital.

I was admitted at the back by a serving-man and taken to the servants' quarters where I proceeded to launch into my quacksalver spiel. But presently I was summoned by the major-domo who ushered me into a long room where an active-looking man with grizzled hair and beard and a humorous eye was pacing up and down.

"Jock Trummle — the lad wi the gowden preens?"

"Aye, Sir David," I confirmed, assuming that this must be he.

"Ah heard tell o ye fae ma freend Sir Richard Maitland o Lethington. There's his letter on the desk; it's got a wee poem aboot yese." His eyes twinkled. "It's no mony packman gets tae be immortalized in Deithless Verse. It's cried 'Fareweel tae Physic'. Here Ah'll read yese a bittie."

And to my mingled embarrassment and amusement, Sir David picked up the letter and solemnly proceeded to declaim the following:

'Gif ye've a fever, aches an pains,
Or ocht that gars ye sick,
Awa wi Physic — there's nae need;

122

He'll cure ye wi a prick …

He looked up at me, sternly trying to suppress a smile. But the effort was too much, and he burst out laughing; I couldn't help joining in.

"We shouldna lauch," said Sir David, still chuckling. "Sir Richard's a fine man an an ornament tae society, but he sud meebe leave the Muse tae ithers. Dinna let on Ah telt ye," he went on in tones of mock alarm, "or Ah'll get ma heid in ma hauns tae plye wi."

After treating a groom of Sir David for diarrhoea, with agaric, and a scullery-maid at the Byres for piles, with ointment prepared from Pellitory-of-the-Wall (two remedies I had learned from the gypsies), I headed north-west to sniff out Luffness and Aberlady. As I walked, I reflected sourly that I was fast becoming that contradiction in terms the well-known spy — Nicholas Wainwright, alias Jock Trummle, 'the lad wi the gowden preens'.

I tried to weigh up the pros and cons concerning Sir David. (His kinsman Lord Lindsay of the Byres had been absent from home.) Like Lord Seton and Sir Richard Maitland, he had been a personal friend of James V. His position as Court Herald made it likely that his sympathies would be royalist and nationalistic. But it was no secret that he was in favour of Church reform, which however did not necessarily make him pro-English, as Wishart and Knox were. I read him as a sturdily independent character who would give his loyalty as his heart and conscience dictated, and not according to any sectarian manifesto or party creed. Tentatively, I included him therefore with the 'Hostiles'.

One small incident occurred as I was leaving Garleton Castle; it didn't seem significant at the time, but I was to recall it later. I observed Sir David emerging from his doocot, and thought in passing that it was a little odd for a nobleman to be engaged in anything so mundane.

'Friendlies' seemed to be limited to the Cockburn family, whose seat was at Ormiston Hall, close to the boundary between East Lothian and Midlothian. Here, George Wishart, Reformer and renegade Scot in the pay of Henry VIII, had been given sanctuary by Alexander Cockburn — a necessary protection, as Wishart was

Number One on Beaton and Bothwell's hit-list.

Thus, two weeks after my arrival in Linton, I had gathered into my hands the main threads of the pattern woven by the Porcupine's creators. Phase Two (Ascham would have called it 'Scouting behind Enemy Lines') was concluded. Phase Three ('Elimination of Target') was now poised to commence.

THE DOOCOT AND THE MILL

SOON, I WAS going to have to mount a 'reconnaissance in depth' of Hailes Castle. The thought of snooping round that grim and gloomy place in its dark defile, gave me a 'cauld grue' as the Scots say. And nothing about the picture I had pieced together of Patrick Hepburn, Earl of Bothwell, made that task seem any more enticing. The problem however, was to be solved in a way I couldn't have foreseen.

But that was in the future. Having completed my reconnaissance of the Theatre, I returned to the Hailes-Markle-Linton triangle, to try to find a base from which to carry out a detailed investigation of that area. I had been toying with the idea of establishing my H.Q. in a barn or in one of Markle's granges — outlying farms visited on a rotational basis by the monks or lay brothers. But by sheer accident, I stumbled — literally, on the perfect solution. Climbing to the top of Dunpender Law, I found (as I had anticipated) an iron basket for a beacon with a stack of firewood ready-cut beside it — an arrangement I had already discovered on the summits of North Berwick Law and the significantly-names Lichter's Law by Pencraik. On the way down, I tripped in a hole. Scrambling to my feet, slightly winded and shaken, I noticed that the side of the hole had fallen away to reveal a tunnel leading back into the hillside. In I crawled to find myself in a stone-lined corridor, three feet high by eight long. It had an indefinable air of being very ancient, and I wondered if it was a souterrain or earthhouse of the Pictish Votadini, whose great hill-fort, according to legend, had once crowned the Law.

Whatever its origins, I realized at once that it would make a perfect hiding-place. I foraged for bracken and had soon made a snug bed inside the place. Water was my only problem; I solved that however when, after foraging in the Tyne below Hailes Castle, I found a discarded ewer (chipped and lacking a handle but quite serviceable as a vessel) capable of holding several pints, and which I could replenish from a burn flowing a short distance below my spy-hole. For food, I laid in a supply of stockfish and winter surplus salt beef, purchased from Sydserff, laird of Ruchlaw — a small estate south-east of Linton, just far enough off, I reckoned, to be safe from 'speiring' tongues. That night, I slept snug and warm on my bed of ferns.

In the morning, I decanted some of my water from the ewer into an empty salve jar for washing and shaving. Then, after a spartan breakfast of stockfish and water, I set out for Linton, first pulling fresh bracken over the mouth of my shelter. I had debated with myself whether or not to take my pack; it would preserve my cover but also slow me down. I decided that mobility was my first priority and left it behind.

Instead of crossing the Tyne, I decided to reconnoitre the town from the bar bank, and followed a path through the laird of Phantassie's cornfields, parallel to a loop of the river running north and south. Ahead, loomed an object like a massive stone beehive — Phantassie doocot. I was about to walk by, when a pigeon flew past me and alighted on the uppermost of the string-courses encircling the building. Something odd about the bird attracted my attention; it seemed to have something fixed to its leg. Bells jangled in my brain, then I recalled George Hepburn and Nicol Crichton, that pair of unlikely ecclesiastics, entering the doocot at Waughton; also Sir David Lindsay coming out of his at Garleton.

Glancing round to make sure I was unobserved, I gripped the lowest of the string courses and began to climb the side of the doocot. Cracks between the stone blocks of its fabric gave me purchase, enabling me to ascend steadily, even if my progress was slow and precarious. The convex curve of the wall was in my favour, and also prevented the pigeon from seeing me.

At last my fingers grasped the topmost string course; gingerly I hauled myself up. The pigeon was sidling along the string course a yard to my left, 'crooing' unconcernedly. A little cylinder of paper or parchment was tied to its leg. Feeling horribly exposed, and also afraid of losing my balance, I released the grip of my left hand and reached out cautiously for the bird. It showed no alarm; life in a doocot would have accustomed it to regular visits by humans I

126

supposed, perhaps it thought I was attempting to feed it. It sidled towards me ... Next moment, my fingers closed on its body and I shoved a pecking, fluttering bundle of indignation inside my shirt. I lost my balance in the process and feeling myself fall, thrust off with my feet and landed clear of the doocot on my back, with a thump that knocked the breath from my body.

Shakily, I got to my feet, immensely relieved to find I had broken no bones. Removing the struggling pigeon from my shirt, I untied the cylinder and shoved the creature into my satchel. I unrolled a tiny strip of parchment covered in the minutest writing you ever saw — far too small to be read without the help of a powerful magnifying glass; one must have been used as an aid to write the message. I rolled it up again, and after retying it to the pigeon's leg, released the bird which flapped up and disappeared through a hole in the sloping roof.

Homing pigeons! — an extremely fast and reliable means of sending information, especially when secrecy was vital. Once again, I was impressed by the boldness and simplicity of the enemy planning; East Lothian, being prime grain country, was thickly dotted with doocots, which, with a little organization, could be transformed into a secure and highly efficient communications network, complemented by the archipelago of beacons, which I had already discovered. So that was five more 'definites' to add to my list of 'Hostiles' — Sir Patrick Hepburn and his son George of Waughton, Nicol Crichton pastor of Prestonhaugh, Sir David Lindsay, and now the Laird of Phantassie.

At last it grew dark enough for me to leave my hiding-place without risk of being observed. I descended from the great willow beside the Tyne where I'd been ensconced for the past three hours, and cautiously walked across the haugh towards Preston Mill. The huddle of buildings dominated by the kiln's distinctively pointed roof, loomed blackly against the stars. Light streamed from a small end window, illuminating the top of the mill wheel, (one of the new undershot kind) so that disembodied dripping paddles rose mysteriously from the darkness into which they disappeared again. The turning wheel prevented my gaining access to that particular window, but a yellow rectangle in the roof showed where there was a dormer window, unshuttered this warm night of early June.

I was counting on the clacking of the wheel and the creak and thump of the machinery to mask the sounds of my feet when I got onto the roof. I had already worked out how I was going to manage this; beside the mill grew a mighty alder, one of whose branches, overhanging the building would provide the means of getting onto the roof. Well, that was the theory ...

Climbing the trunk with its knobbly projections and rough bark was no problem. I wormed my way along the branch until I was poised several feet above the roof. Suddenly the pitch of the pantiles looked horribly steep, and I felt sweat break out between my shoulder blades. I had enough sense to realize that if I sat there dithering, I would stick, so, hanging onto the limb with both hands, I swung myself down and dropped. My feet jarred on the tiles; for a moment I teetered and almost fell the wrong way, then I managed to fling myself sideways against the roof, my hands clawing desperately for purchase before I should slide off. I felt myself slipping, then my scrabbling fingers found the roof-ridge and clutched it with the strength of desperation. I waited till the wild thumping of my heart had eased, and until I was sure that the sound of my landing hadn't been heard above the rumbling machinery. Then I pulled myself along the roof-ridge until I was beside the dormer window.

The projecting embrasure gave me solid support for which I was enormously thankful; I clung to it getting my breath back and allowing my tense nerves to relax, for all these acrobatics combined with nervous strain had begun to tax my reserves. When I had recovered somewhat, I craned my neck and peeped in through the window.

I was looking onto the upper floor of the mill. Instead of feed hoppers, elevators, shelling and grinding stones, what I saw were drills — powered by driving wheels, connected by endless belts to the complex gearing system of the mill. Operated by shirt-sleeved men, their faces set in concentration, some drill-bits were biting into long steel cylinders, which I thought could only be gun-barrels; others were boring multiple perforations in squat steel drums,

128

whose purpose I couldn't imagine. A thrill of exultation surged through me; I had no doubt at all that I was witnessing the manufacture of components of the Porcupine.

I dropped from the roof, landing softly in thick grass, and hurried back towards base. For the first time in my quest, the lineaments of the Porcupine itself were becoming visible. I think I understood something of what Theseus must have felt as he drew near to the Minotaur in the labyrinth. As I travelled I summed up my findings about the Porcupine. Ammunition components — these were being prepared at Lethington and perhaps the Abbey's Gimmers Mills at Haddington, prior to assembly and packaging at the Abbey. This supposition, strictly, was guesswork, but the circumstantial evidence was so strong that I was certain it was correct. Preston Mill was drilling gun-barrels and other parts, and I felt sure that other local mills must be engaged in similar activity. I wondered fleetingly if this would disrupt the local food-supply, then dismissed the thought. Central government — the final authority for the organization of the Porcupine's manufacture, would surely set up a subsidy system. How many mills I wondered, had been converted to armaments factories? The vales of Tyne and Peffer were 'fair thrang wi mills' to quote Gibbie Cochrane; Preston Mill was probably the key plant, but there could well be a number of subsidiary ones. Using machine-driven tools, components could be produced en masse and with the necessary degree of precision.

Where did Hailes and Markle fit into the picture? Tomorrow, I would make a start on finding out the answer by paying another visit to Markle. And after Markle — Hailes Castle and Patrick Hepburn. The Big H. My stomach contracted at the thought.

THE BIG H

THE FOLLOWING DAY, I set off for Markle via Linton, pack on back — the travelling quacksalver once more. Markle township was too small a community for me to be able to snoop around without attracting attention, and the security of the monastic buildings would be too tight probably for me to risk any form of secret spying. My only possible stratagem seemed to be a frontal assault as Jock Trummle, peddler of salves — which, monks invariably being skilled physicians, was rather like trying to sell ice to the Greenlanders. I would just have to keep my senses well honed and hope to pick up something.

But fate had other plans in store for me. Stepping into Gibbie Cochrane's 'fur tae hear the clash' as the Scots put it, whom should I encounter but Ecky Tait, his cheerful red face half-hidden in a quart mug.

"Weel met Jock," he called out cheerily. "Come an sit ye doon an gie's yeir crack. Gibbie — the same again fur Jock here. Man — Ah've been speirin a ower fur yese. Wait till ye hear fur why." He paused expectantly and I asked on cue, "Go on — tell me."

"Ye'll never ken whae it is wants tae see ye," he went on, clearly bent on squeezing every drop of drama from his undisclosed revelation.

"Prioress Elizabeth?" I suggested, drawing a bow at a venture.

"Like eneuch she'd welcome some mair treatment fur — 'the back' wis it? Heh! Heh! But it's no her. Try again."

"Oh I expect it's Arran," I said airily. "Or the Earl o Bothwell, perhaps."

Ecky's jaw dropped. "Noo how the hell did ye —? Och Ah see, it's jist yeir bit joke. But ye're richt fur a that. Twa days syne when Ah wis at the Castle, Lord Hailes himsel cas me in. 'Ecky,' says he, 'Ah hae tane a fancy fur tae see this traivellin quacksalver Ah hear tell o — him that's supposed tae cure fowks wi stickin preens intae them. Ah'm telt ye ken the lad. Ah want fur ye tae fetch him here.'

130

Man — it seems ye're gettin tae be famous. Ah'm richt glad Ah've fand ye, Ah can tell ye. When His Grace asks ye fur tae dae somethin, it's best ye dae it."

Here at a stroke was my entrée to Hailes Castle. I should have been overjoyed; my reaction was nearer to panic.

I whistled to show that I was pleased, as this was what Ecky clearly expected. "An invitation by His Grace the Earl o Bothwell — now that really *is* something. First, I've just got some business in Markle to — "

"Then it'll hae tae wait," Ecky broke in grimly. "Man, have Ah no jist been tellin ye — when Lord Hailes says 'jump', then ye jump. So drink up Jock lad, an we'll be fur aff."

At the Castle gatehouse, I was passed on to the captain of the guard, who handed Ecky a purse — presumably a tip from Lord Hailes should Ecky be successful in his search for me. (The expression 'bounty money' slipped unbidden into my mind. Get a grip Wainwright and stop panicking, I told myself savagely).

Leaving my pack in the gatehouse, but retaining my satchel, I was conducted through the curtain wall, across a courtyard, contained on the north side by a long range of buildings, of dates varying from one to three hundred years ago I guessed, and dominated by two towers, one at the western end and the other in the middle. A noise like farriers at work issued from a chapel-like building between the towers. I was led up a flight of spiral stairs in the older block to the east of the central tower. My escort knocked at a door, ushered me in at the same time calling out, "The quacksalver, Yeir Grace," then departed, shutting the door behind him.

I was in a long room, whose massively functional thirteenth century construction, contrasted with modern additions — fireplace, enlarged windows, rich tapestries and Turkey rugs. There were touches of odd luxury — a profusion of finely-made furniture of continental workmanship, knick-knacks such as clocks and mirrors, and, a bizarre touch, a tiny marmoset monkey that capered among the chairs and tables.

In the midst of all this almost feminine refinement, towered the massive figure of the Earl of Bothwell. Patrick Hepburn was a huge,

131

coarsely-handsome man, with wavy auburn hair and full moustaches above a closely-trimmed beard. He stared at me appraisingly and I was immediately aware of a powerful aura surrounding the man, a sheer animal strength and vitality, as palpable as the scent emanating from a vase of roses on an inlaid table beside me.

"So — ye're the lad whae sticks preens in a body tae cure them." Although Hepburn's voice was pleasantly modulated and polite, I imagined I detected an underlying hint of mockery and menace, an impression pointed up by the fact that he clearly thought me of so little personal account as not to bother to enquire what my name was.

"I've had a crash course in the theory, that's a Yeir Grace," I replied. "I've only treated but the yin patient so far."

"Successfully?"

"I believe so, Yeir Grace."

"He believes so," Hepburn repeated, his voice even more softly polite, so that the mockery showed nakedly through. The marmoset landed on his shoulder, and he began stroking it absently. "Thon's nae answer. Nae sort of answer ava. Speak plain lad."

"Well — yes. The treatment was successful."

Suddenly a wave of fear and apprehension seemed to wash over me. I have sometimes been tempted to wonder since, if it was premonition, although reason tells me otherwise. Perhaps it was the accumulating strain of my dangerous solo job, that — although I had not really been tested yet, was beginning to tell on me. Or perhaps it was the aura of threat which seemed to surround this man. Aristocratic birth and foreign travel had given Patrick Hepburn a poise and polish that concealed, I felt, a nature unprincipled and violent. I began to feel that I was walking on a mere crust of solid ground covering a treacherous quicksand.

"Ah have anither patient fur ye." Hepburn poured wine from a chased silver flagon into a blue Venetian glass, and downed it in a single swallow. "Tell me quacksalver — dae ye ken ocht o witch-craft?"

Witchcraft! The question was so unexpected and its implications so sinister, that I was unable to reply for several seconds. I began to

132

wonder if Hepburn were mentally unbalanced. What *did* I know about witchcraft? Almost nothing, beyond the fact that in Germany, egged on by Martin Luther, persecution of witches had been growing, I'd heard. I wasn't even sure that I knew what witchcraft actually was; it involved some sort of pact with the Devil, I thought, but I couldn't be certain.

I shook my head. "Nothing, Yeir Grace."

"Guid," said Hepburn, enigmatically. He poured and drank more wine. "Ah've a wumman held in the Castle, accused o witchcraft. Ah want fur ye tae find oot if there's ony pairt o her she disna feel an which disna bleed when ye prick it."

The matter-of-fact tone in which Hepburn announced this, made the statement all the more incredible and horrible. All at once, perhaps as a reaction to my fear, I found myself becoming very angry. That this man should assume that I would compliantly agree to torture a helpless prisoner, as though my own conscience and free-will did not matter, was outrageous.

"Wi respect, Yeir Grace, ye can go to Hell," I heard myself reply. "I'll no be any party to yeir sadistic little schemes."

Suddenly I was appalled at the enormity of my indiscretion; I waited for the storm to burst. But Hepburn seemed completely unperturbed. "As ye will, quacksalver," he said equably, looking at me as though he suddenly found me interesting. "Come wi me. Whit ye're aboot tae see will mebbe mak ye change yeir mind."

Brushing the marmoset from his shoulder, he preceded me down the stairs, through a hall and into the basement of the central tower. An opened hatchway in the floor allowed me a glimpse into a dark pit lined with stone blocks.

"The better o wur twa prisons," remarked Hepburn carelessly. (God, what was the *other* like?)

I followed Hepburn up a stair into the first floor chamber, furnished as a living-room. I stared in horror at the figure in the centre of the room.

A young woman, naked, was seated on a chair to which she was bound by her wrists. Her shaven head was encased in a nightmarish sort of head-mask of iron strapwork, that put me in mind of a muzzle for a dangerous brute. Apart from Hepburn and myself, there were three other people in the room — a burly guard, an elderly man who from his habit must be a monk or friar, and a brutal-looking menial in darned hose and greasy leather jerkin.

"We can only prove her guilt or innocence the yin wye," Hepburn said to me. "Gif there's a spot where she disna feel ocht an which disna bleed when ye prick it — that shows the Deil's touched her there, an she's guilty. (The fact that he was bothering to explain this to me, showed I thought, that I had risen in his estimation — probably as a result of my little outburst). If no — then she's innocent. When Ah heard tell o ye an yeir gowden preens, Ah thocht tae masel, here's the verra lad tae settle the maitter."

"It's sheer barbarity!" I exclaimed. "I'll no have anything to do wi it." I knew now that to stand up to Hepburn boldly was the only way to avoid being stamped into the ground.

Hepburn shrugged and nodded at the gaoler, for such I guessed the menial to be.

The man grinned, showing discoloured broken teeth, and drew from his jerkin a long, sharp-looking brass pin. He approached the bound woman and proceeded to scrutinize her naked body, in a horrible gloating possessive kind of way — a gruesome travesty of a surgeon deciding where to make his incision. The woman started to tremble. I felt sick with revulsion and helpless rage. Even the guard, a case-hardened veteran if ever I saw, shifted and looked uncomfortable.

Suddenly, the man's hand thrust forward and the pin drove to the head, into her breast. The woman jerked, and strained against her bonds; harrowing noises issued from behind the muzzle. A thread of blood trickled from beneath the pin head.

A red mist seemed to gather in front of my eyes. I found myself crossing the floor and my fist, seemingly of its own volition, slammed into the gaoler's face sending him sprawling on the floor.

Then my arms were grabbed and pinioned behind me, and I was dragged back. I struggled helplessly in the guard's iron grip.

With a snarl, the gaoler staggered to his feet, wiping blood from his pulped lips and spitting out a tooth — which gave me a throb of satisfaction.

"Cairry on," said Hepburn, as though nothing had happened.

The monk had remained impassive throughout.

Giving me a wary glance, to make sure I was securely held I suppose, the creature retrieved his pin and advancing on his victim once more, thrust it into the soft flesh of her shoulder. Again the convulsive reaction, the muffled cry of agony.

"Ye inhuman bastards!" I yelled. "Ye'll kill her before ye've decided whether she's guilty or innocent. But I don't suppose that matters. And what have ye done to her mouth?"

"Jist a bit spike ower her tongue," said Hepburn nonchalantly. "So she canna drink. Gin she's a witch, she's supposed tae be able tae thole ony treatment gif she can get but a sip o water."

Four more times, I watched the hideous performance repeated. Then I knew that I could stand no more.

"Call him off," I cried. "I'll take over." I reckoned that by using the Chinese needles, the risk of her being proved guilty was certainly no greater than if she continued to be subjected to this monster's ministrations. Indeed, with my knowledge (theoretical admittedly) of the meridians and sensitive points, I might even be able to establish her innocence. And the fine golden needles would cause her only mild discomfort, compared to the excruciating pain inflicted by the brass bodkin. (I thought of Operation Porcupine and decided I needed this nightmarish complication like I needed a hole in the head.)

My pack was brought from the gatehouse; taking out the case of golden needles, I moved over to the bound figure. "I promise I'll no hurt ye," I said, trying to sound reassuring. Feeling myself to be in a sense master of the situation, I proceeded to indulge in a little muscle-flexing.

"As I seem to be both Counsel for the Defence and for the Prosecution," I declared, "We'll do things my way. Presumably this is supposed to be a courtroom, no a torture chamber, so as a first step I insist that the prisoner be untied."

Hepburn nodded at the gaoler who reluctantly released her bonds.

"Secondly, I want yon — thing, removed from her head. Wi a ye able-bodied men around, I hardly think she's going to be taking any illicit sips o water."

Again Hepburn nodded. The gaoler selected a small key from the bunch at his belt, and fitted it into a padlock securing a hasp at the back of the muzzle.

The woman's hand moved forward and closed on mine, with a peculiar urgency. Was she thanking me? I wondered, or clinging for comfort to someone who offered a ray of hope? Not till it was too late, did I realize that it was a warning that she was trying to communicate.

There was a click, and the horrible cage confining the woman's head was lifted clear. Unbelievingly, I stared at the familiar features which were revealed to me.

"Wattie!"

The ejaculation was ripped from me involuntarily. Filled with pain and despair, Wattie's eyes stared into mine; I went hot and cold with horror as I realized that the uttering of those two syllables, by revealing our association had sealed the fate not only of Wattie (if that had not already been decided) and myself, but of Operation Porcupine.

In a sort of dream, I heard Hepburn say, "Tak her back tae the pit." And to myself, in a mildly surprised, almost admiring tone, "Weel, whae'd hae thocht it — twa birds wi the yin stane."

STIGMATA SAGARUM

MY SATCHEL was removed; I was made to strip, when my money-belt was taken away also. Then I was allowed to dress again. (I reminded myself that the only bits of incriminating evidence I possessed — the brass cartridge case and my map, were back in my base where I'd been careful to leave them, against just such an eventuality as this. They'd no proof. As if they needed it, I told myself, realising that I was just whistling in the dark.)

So Wattie was a woman after all! Despite the evidence of my senses, my mind refused to equate the swaggering lad with the caustic tongue I'd ruffled with in Edinburgh, and the stricken girl I had just seen treated with such degrading cruelty. Waves of anger, shame and pity washed over me, to be followed by a fierce determination to somehow help my friend whatever the cost, should any opportunity to do so occur. I tried to think of Wattie as 'her' but my mind rejected the concept utterly, insisting that the woman I had seen was a stranger whose face was in his likeness. With a huge effort I got the tumult of my conflicting emotions under control; to have the slightest chance of getting out of this one, my mind must remain as cold as ice, my nerves as steady as Dunpender Law.

Dismissing the guard with an injunction to bring wine and writing materials, Hepburn stretched out in a wooden armchair, his long legs crossed, and told the monk to be seated at the room's only table.

"Sit ye doon on thon creepie, lad," he said expansively, indicating a three-legged stool. "Ye're mebbe no exactly a gentleman — nae gentleman wad be a spy, but ye're somethin like a man." I seemed to detect a note almost of approval in his voice. He went on, "Ye're in a kittle bit, lad. Yeir freend wis tane fower days back. Caught snoopin aboot inside o Fawside Castle — thon's atween Musselburgh an Tranent, an is yin o wur storage depots. The ithers are Broughty Castle, Inchcolm, the Castle o Milk, an Home

137

Castle. We wis fair dumfoonered whan we had the claes affa him an fand he wis a she. A bonnie lass an a brave forbye. But braw looks an high mettle willna save her. Ah offered her a clean death an a quick, gif she was tell me a she kent. But she'll say nocht."

By this time, I had recovered sufficiently to make some attempt to fight back.

"Look — what's all this about?" I protested, trying to inject a note of puzzled outrage into my voice. "You've nothing you can hold me on. That girl reminded me of someone I once knew called Wattie. We can all make mistakes." Even as I uttered them, the words sounded absurdly unconvincing in my own ears. And, I realized with sick self-disgust, such was my agitation that they had been delivered in the 'received pronunciation' of the King's English with no attempt to give them a Scottish intonation!

Hepburn's hoot of amusement was confirmation of my total rout.

"But — witchcraft," I objected, conceding defeat. "Where on earth does that come in?" Hepburn's cheerful disclosure of confidential information was ominous I thought. He would hardly be telling it to someone who was going to be around to pass it on. Clearly Wattie was a spy. With a brief flare of anger against Ascham and Co., I wondered if part of his (her) brief had been to keep tabs on myself. Whatever the answer to that one was, Wattie must have gone on to carry out independent investigations, presumably concerning the Porcupine.

The wine and the writing materials arrived, and Hepburn dismissed the guard. Clearly he entertained no fears about being able to handle me, should I attempt to escape. Looking at his huge body lounging in the chair, I sensed the man's enormous latent strength and knew that any bid for freedom on my part would be a doomed effort. He put me in mind of a great lazy lion. (He did however pay me the compliment of checking that his dagger moved sweetly in its sheath).

Hepburn took two goblets from a cupboard and filled them with wine. To my surprise, he offered one to myself, but did not extend the same courtesy to the monk. Whether it was just his whim to treat me with friendly confidentiality, or whether I had won a degree of standing for myself in his opinion, I had no means of telling. Perhaps, when he had tired of playing with me, I would be brushed aside, like the marmoset. Meanwhile, my best course of action was probably to try to hold his interest, keep him engaged in talk. I might learn something which I could turn to my advantage, In all likelihood, I would only be spinning out the inevitable, but it was the only card I had and I was going to play it for all it was worth.

"Witchcraft," said Hepburn speculatively. Downing his wine at a gulp, he refilled his goblet, telling me to help myself when I was ready. "Ach — a lot o auld wife's havers, gin ye ask me. It's a pit-up job fur Arran's benefit."

"Your Grace?"

"It's a lang story. Dae ye want fur tae hear it?"

"Assuredly, Your Grace."

"Syne the Spring, Scotland's been fair deaved wi English spies." Hepburn settled himself more comfortably in his chair, tossed off his wine and poured more. "You an the lassie bring the total up tae fower athegither that's been caught. Ah wis fur hingin the ither twa, but Arran wadna hae it. 'Na, na, Patrick,' he said in thon snivellin whine o his. 'Ye're no tae kill them. Ah ken Anglo-Scottish relations is no jist exactly whit ye'd cry cordial the noo, but times can change. King Henry'd no be best pleased gin we killit his secret envoys.'" Hepburn chuckled and shook his head.

"'Secret envoys' — noo Ah've heard it a, says Ah tae masel. 'So ye're jist tae lock them up Patrick, safe an soond' says he, waggin his finger at me like a dominie, 'till a this blaws ower.' The fushionless gowk!"

"Aweel — Arran's the boss, so, like he said Ah didna kill them. Ah jist fixit that their clackin tongues wad speir nae mair. An pit them in a place that's safer nor only gyle, an where naebody will ever come fur tae let them oot."

"I know," I said. "Leper houses."

"Ye fand thon oot?" Again that hint of admiration in Hepburn's voice. "Man, as a spy ye fairly ken yeir business. Did yese gang inside o yin?"

"Yes — the one near Calton Hill."

"Then by Christ, ye've mair smeddum nor me — Ah'm no

139

'shamed tae own it." Hepburn shuddered. "The verra thocht o yin o thae places gies me the cauld grue. The ither spy's in St Lawrence's lazar-hoose ootside o Haddington."

Ruthless though it was, I couldn't help admitting that Hepburn's solution was an original and effective one.

"A brilliant idea, Your Grace," I conceded. "Why change to charges of withcraft?"

"The wye things is gaun, we'd soon rin oot o lazar hooses," replied Hepburn with a wry grin. "'sides, when we caught yeir lady freend, Ah kent things wis gettin past a joke. Ah decided Ah wad hae tae settle her hash, an that o ony mair spies, for guid — but in a wye that Arran wadna be able tae quarrel wi. Ah telt him three spies in a raw didna seem natural-like; perhaps they wis in league wi the Deil fur tae speir oot Scotland's Muckle Secret. The daft auld runt hauf-believed me, an wis fly eneuch forbye fur tae see that here wis a let-oot. When the clash got back tae England that spies wad be tryit fur witches, they'd mebbe no be sae keen fur tae come. 'Jist see that it's a done legal-like, Patrick,' says Arran, handing ower the dirty wark tae me as per usual."

"What *is* the legal position?" I asked, fascinated despite myself.

"Faither Ignatius here kens mair aboot thon nor me. That's why he's here — tae see it's 'a done legal-like'. Explain tae him, Faither."

The monk, who so far had been fiddling abstractedly with his pen, sighed impatiently, his smooth authoritative features puckered with irritation.

"I think it hardly necessary Your Grace, to enlarge on these matters for the benefit of a common spy," he said.

"Dae ye indeed?" purred Hepburn in his softest voice. "Ye may be cock o the midden fur a Ah ken in Holyrood Faither, but Ah'll remind ye it's Patrick Hepburn's the maister here. Thon girdle at yeir waist — gin it's twistit roon yeir heid a bittie, Ah'll guarantee ye'll speak mair ceevil-like."

"No need for that Your Grace," said the monk hurriedly, his bland features turning pale. Licking his lips, he turned to me.

"The legal position's a bit ticklish," he said, in precise lawyer-like tones. "We don't actually have a Statute against witchcraft in Scotland — yet. Mind you, it'll probably come if these dreadful

140

Reformers have their way. Look what's happening in Germany. It's always the same with a revolutionary movement; once in power they enforce conformity, often by means of a Reign of Terror. Take for example —"

"Stop haverin man, an get on wi it," interrupted Hepburn.

"We can really only go back sixty years," the monk continued hurriedly. "1484 to be precise, when Pope Innocent VIII published 'Summis desiderantes affectibus' to counter a current craze for devil-worship in Germany."

"Joan of Arc?" I objected.

"Oh that," retorted Father Ignatius dismissively. "A regrettable piece of political jobbery. Quite exceptional. They'll probably get around to making her a saint one of these centuries. Anyway, shortly after 'Summis desiderantes', a couple of rogues — Sprenger and Kramer, brought out 'Malleus Maleficarum', a sort of do-it-yourself handbook for detecting witches. Been a best-seller ever since in Germany, where witchcraft is now being prosecuted with the full rigour of the law."

"And in Scotland?"

"Up till now, witchcraft's been a total non-issue, though as I've suggested, that may not last. In 1510 a Justice Ayre in Jedburgh made some enquiries about whether sorcery existed in Scotland. In 1536 a certain Agnes Scott was convicted at Aberdeen of being a witch, but got let off with a caution, if memory serves me right. In 1537 Lady Douglas was burned as a witch on the Castlehill in Edinburgh for plotting the death of James V, but that was really a political frame-up. Then three years ago, some witches from Edinburgh and Dunfermline were burned at St Andrews, but without proper authority. And that's about all the track record there is to go on. Whether there's any strictly legal grounds for prosecuting someone for witchcraft as such, is doubtful. Up till the present, it's usually been necessary to prove association with heresy or murder, for a witchcraft charge to stick."

"So — how do you get round it?"

"Nae problem," broke in Hepburn, who had been listening to this exposition with an air of amusement. "Ah've gotten a Special Commission fae the Privy Council. As Sherrif o East Lothian Ah'm empowered by the Commission tae prosecute a suspeckit witch, where witchcraft is thocht tae hae been used tae hairm the State."

"Neat," I murmured with reluctant admiration. "What actually constitutes the offence of witchcraft with which the accused is charged?"

"We're on rather stronger ground here," said Father Ignatius. "Witchcraft consists of soliciting the power of the Evil One or his representatives for the accomplishment of *any* purpose — benign or otherwise. Proof that a compact with the Evil One has been entered into is, as His Grace has already pointed out, the finding of a place on the suspect's body that is insensitive to feeling and which does not bleed. Unfortunately, this involves the painful technique of 'pricking'. This spot is held to be the place where the Devil has touched the suspect with his finger, to seal the compact."

"And you believe that!"

"Whether I believe it or not, isn't relevant," said Father Ignatius with a wintry smile. "I'm simply here as an impartial witness on behalf of the Privy Council to see that the trial is carried out in accordance with the law."

A wave of weary disgust at the whole cooked-up charade swept over me. And yet in all fairness, I couldn't wholly condemn Bothwell for his scheme. By his lights, I suppose, he was only doing his patriotic duty. His country was in deadly peril (I could hardly expect him to understand that for Scotland to submerge her national identity with that of England, would be to the advantage of both peoples) and desperate situations call for desperate measures. From a Nationalist viewpoint, Scotland needed strong decisive men like Beaton and Bothwell, not well-meaning weaklings like Arran who, if he had not been checked by more resolute minds, would have sold Scotland down the river to Henry.

"The penalty, if the charge is proved?" I asked. A wild fluttering started up at the base of my stomach.

"The witch's body must be consumed utterly by fire — so that no trace of her, or his evil influence can remain," said Father Ignatius. "I suppose the ultimate authority is the injunction in Holy Scripture, 'Thou shalt not suffer a witch to live.' As an act of mercy, the witch is usually strangled before burning, but that's up

142

to the presiding authorities. Again, a confession is desirable, but the Devil's mark — the 'Stigmata Sagarum' is generally accepted per se as proof positive."

"And you're going to make sure you find that mark," I said bitterly.

"O course we are," said Bothwell, and added, not unsympathetically, "Ye can surely see fur why, lad."

So it wasn't going to make any difference in the end, whether the gaoler or myself did the 'pricking', I reflected bitterly, as I paced the chamber, alone but for the solitary guard by the door. 'Wattie' was marked for death — an unimaginably agonising death unless 'he' (try as I might I couldn't think of Wattie as 'she') was allowed the privilege of being strangled first. That was unlikely I thought; the object of the exercise was to deter would-be spies, and burning alive would certainly be a more effective deterrent than mere strangling. When news filtered back of Wattie's hideous death, I couldn't imagine queues of applicants rushing to fill the vacancy.

A chilling thought struck me. So far I had been preoccupied about Wattie's fate. But would my own be any different? The answer had to be that it would not. Death by fire. I recalled the agony of the candle-flame against my palm in 'The Garter' in Windsor, and my mouth dried out with terror.

The subsequent train of events seemed like a nightmare travesty of a play. The 'interval' over, the 'audience' — Hepburn and Father Ignatius, took their seats, and the 'actors' — the gaoler, preceded by Wattie, made their entrance. At least Hepburn had had the decency to waive the requirement that Wattie wear the obscene witch's bridle. I noted with mingled horror and fury, the angry red dots on her naked body where the pin had been driven home.

"I'm sorry Wattie," I said miserably as she passed me.

She stopped and smiled at me — a smile of tender resignation. "Not your fault, Jock," she said, and I was thrown by her voice. There was no trace of Scottish accent — instead a soft Northumbrian burr, so different from the harsh sing-song of the speech to the north side of the Border line. "You did well. Our luck ran out, that's all."

143

With feelings akin to shock and disorientation, I realized that the Wattie I had known — the boon companion, the devil-may-care young blade with his touchy pride that was somehow endearing, no longer existed, never had existed in fact. 'Wattie' had been a mere persona, projected by a consummately skilled professional.

Very pale, but dignified despite her nakedness and shaven head, Wattie walked composedly to the chair in the centre and sat down. The gaoler made to tie her, but she appealed to Hepburn; "There is no need. I'm not going to run away."

Hepburn shrugged, gave a wry half-smile and shook his head at the gaoler. As the man stood hesitating, Wattie's hand suddenly flashed out and whipped the brass pin from his jerkin. Before anyone had had time to react, she had plunged it deep into the flesh of her upper arm. ('Stappit the preen in her ain airm richt tae the heid', as I heard the guard put it, to one of his companions later.)

"Let us put an end to this farce, Your Grace," Wattie called in a clear steady voice. "Look — no blood. And I don't feel a thing. You're got your Devil's Mark. Satisfied?"

The monk's pen squeaked eagerly.

A shaft of late sunlight beamed through the window, bathing her naked body in a mellow light, and causing the brazen pin head in her arm to blaze like gold. Very straight and proud she sat, transfigured for a few fleeting moments into a queen upon a throne. An overwhelming surge of pity and admiration washed over me.

"By God, but ye're a brave lass!" exclaimed Hepburn, and I think even that hard man was moved. "Ah'll speak ye plain. Ah'll gie ye yin mair chance tae tell us a ye ken — contacts, safe hooses, information ye've fand oot an passed on aboot the Muckle Secret. Come on — speak lass. Death by fire; thon's a bad wye tae go. Ah'll gie ye fur as lang as thon sunbeam lasts."

A profound silence fell in the chamber. With a thumping heart, I watched the glowing shaft march steadily across the room, flame briefly against the window embrasure, vanish. A sigh of expelled breath ended the silence.

"Ah didna think ye'd speak," said Hepburn quietly. "Ah'm sorry it has tae be this wye lass." The pen, and the confession which the monk had been writing out, were passed to her. She signed.

144

Hepburn signalled to the gaoler, who escorted her out. He dismissed the others then turned to me.

"Ye're tae be cell-mates. Ye'll hae plenty o time tae talk wi her, get her tae see sense." Patrick Hepburn spoke roughly, and I didn't think it was just the failure to elicit information from Wattie that troubled him. "Gin ye can get her tae change her mind, an the baith o ye tell us a ye ken, Ah gie ye ma word as a gentleman that yeir lives will be spared. Ah'll bide till the morn's morn afore Ah send aff the confession tae the Privy Cooncil in Embro. Until he gets it, Arran'll no sign the Death Warrant. The Warrant canna get here till the efternin at earliest. So the execution will be the day efter the morn." He looked at me grimly. "Then we stert on ye, lad." He paused to let the import of the words sink in, then went on, "Ah'll hae tae pit yese in the ither prison; ma lads has jist tane some o Hertford's Riders an they maun gang in the auld pit, that's bigger."

Hepburn shouted for the guard; I was escorted out of the central tower into the courtyard, where we were joined by the gaoler, past the chapel into the western tower. Here, in the north wall, the gaoler opened an iron trap-door, revealing a stone-lined pit similar to the other, but smaller. Picking up a coil of rope, he lowered it part of the way through the entry, then instructed me to put my foot in the bottom loop and to hold on. I was lowered down into the dark depths. The gaoler let go before I reached bottom; but I was ready for such a trick (remembering how I had served him at the 'trial') and landed without mishap. The rope was drawn up and I heard above me the grille clang shut, and the rasp of the bolt being slammed home.

IN THE PIT

"JOCK?"

"Wattie," I answered, groping in the direction of the voice. I was in a tiny vaulted chamber. Dimly, I could make out Wattie, clad in shirt and hose, crouched against the wall. At least we weren't in darkness as I'd feared we might be; the light of gloaming filtered down a ventilator shaft opening into the west wall of this horrible den, and also through a circular garderobe in the north wall. So at least the air was pure and, being warmed a little by the sunlight, made the place less dank and chill than I expected it would be.

Instinctively, I moved to put my arms round Wattie — then hesitated. The shaven head and man's clothes she was wearing, coupled with my own memories and images, set up an immovable blockage preventing me from thinking of her as a woman. She solved the problem in a direct and practical way. Taking my hands in hers she guided them to her breasts. Wonderingly, I explored her body, the knowledge of my fingertips gradually building a new and three-dimensional image, until I had created a different, female person from the Wattie I remembered. It was a strange and thrilling experience, akin to that of Pygmalion, I thought. She put her lips to my ear and whispered, "It's Helen."

With the words, the transformation was complete; 'Wattie' was sloughed away, as completely as its old skin is sloughed off by a snake. The barriers crumbled and we were in each other's arms, drawing comfort from the contact of our bodies, feeling the pain and terror of the past hours dissolve away.

I surfaced slowly from profound unconsciousness. For a moment, I was disorientated, then I felt Helen stir beside me and memory flooded back — a mosaic of terrifying images.

It was dark and the air was chill, but a little dawn light was filtering into the chamber through the garderobe. As I massaged some warmth into my stiff limbs, Helen sat up beside me.

"Listen Helen," I said, "there's a way out of this mess." And I told her about the proposition which Hepburn had made to me. As I spoke, it seemed that youth had never appeared sweeter, that life unrolled before us like a golden highway. And for the price of a few words, we could step out upon that highway. 'England' seemed like a shadowy abstraction, an insubstantial wraith that it would be madness to die for. No one could expect in fairness, more from us than what we had already given. She clung to me and I held her trembling body close.

But she was strong, stronger than I was. She gave a long sigh, then whispered, 'No'.

As hope died, I felt possessed by a strange calm. The execution would not be till tomorrow, so we had a day in which to explore possible avenues of escape. But looking at the massive ashlar of the pit prison, I felt escape to be hopeless. Even if I could reach the trap-door, it would surely be impossible to push it back, as it was secured by a bolt. Still, we may as well investigate.

"Why not?" Helen said with a smile, when I put the suggestion. "It'll pass the time."

We waited until the gaoler let us have our food — a bucket lowered at the end of a rope containing to my surprise, besides a loaf of bread and a can of water, a cold fowl and a flagon of wine — the latter obviously on Bothwell's orders. We removed the provender and the bucket was drawn up. Down clanged the hatch and the bolt smacked home.

I knelt down and Helen straddled my neck. Then slowly I stood upright, lifting Helen pick-a-back so that she could reach the trap. She felt with her fingers through the grille to see if she could reach the bolt

"It's no good," she called down. "The bolt must run behind this wide bar in the middle. There's no way I can reach it."

I stopped and she clambered down from my shoulders. "Well — at least we tried, Nick." she murmured. (I had of course told her my real name by this time.)

It was almost a relief to know that there was nothing else that we could do. All that remained was to hope that some outside agency might intervene on our behalf — Hertford's Riders might thunder up over the horizon and storm Hailes, Arran might have another change of heart and agree to the Royal Marriage, Bothwell might be thrown from his horse and break his neck; pigs might fly.

Muffled by the thick stonework, a distant clinking din started up that reminded me of the noise I had heard coming from the chapel, when I had arrived at the Castle. (This noise was to continue during daylight hours all the time I remained in the pit.)

As we shared the meal, Helen told me about her past life. She had been born in 1522 (the year of my own birth) into a branch of the Grahams — a prominent Border tribe, mainly settled in north Northumberland. Owing to a boundary adjustment in her grandfather's time, the Border line actually ran through the peel tower which was the family stronghold. Helen had been delivered literally on the line.

"I was born with my head in England and my feet in Scotland," she laughed, "so that made me English."

"But only just!" I objected. "No offence meant Helen — if you tell me you're a true-blue Englishwoman, all right I'll believe you. But could Ascham, in his position, have afforded to take you on trust? You have to admit, your origins do seem a bit ambivalent."

Helen smiled. "I can't blame you for wondering. It may surprise you, but our branch of the Grahams is one of the most staunchly patriotic of English families."

"Tell me," I asked, sensing there was a story behind this bald statement.

"Well, back in 1401, Henry IV led an army in person on a raid against the Scots — the last English king to do so, by the way. Failing to take Edinburgh Castle, the English fell back and were routed in a surprise attack led by Archibald fourth Earl of Douglas at, guess where? — just outside where we are now, below Pencraik Hill. A Graham of our sept was hard-pressed in the fighting, by several Scots. Hearing his cry for help, King Henry with two knights charged the Scots and drove them off. From that day on my family took as its motto 'Leal to the King' and since then has never borne arms in a Scottish cause."

"No wonder Ascham felt he could trust you," I murmured impressed by the strange little tale, which had helped to clear up the last traces of enigma surrounding the Wattie-Helen story.

148

Her formative years had been passed against an exciting and violent background of forays, hot trods, and skirmishes on both sides of the Border, her own family, in marked contrast to the Graham tendency to switch sides when it suited, invariably identifying with the English and not the Scottish reivers of the Graham surname. Spirited and tomboyish, she had more than once in her early teens played a man's part in the defence of the tower, with pike and hackbut. At about this time, she had discovered a natural flair for organization, and had gradually taken over the management of the estate, coping with accounts, ordering supplies, managing the business correspondence, and at times riding to Newcastle or Carlisle representing the family interests in lawsuits and business arrangements.

"Good for you," I said admiringly, "but with respect, surely as a woman you wouldn't carry enough clout to be effective in negotiations away from home. In law, a married woman's pretty well the chattel of her husband; even a spinster finds it difficult to be a free agent when it comes to running her own affairs."

"True, unfortunately. Mind you, things are beginning to improve slowly. In Italy, women tend to be accepted in intellectual circles on an equal footing with men — take Isabella d'Este Gonzaga for instance; in Scotland, Mary of Guise runs rings round most of the rest of the Council, giving the lie to that old Adam's rib nonsense. I got round the problem to some extent by tending to dress as a man when I was conducting business outside the home." Helen smiled reminiscently. "That was a fantastic discovery. As a man, I found a whole new world of fun and freedom opening up for me, and I began to 'cross over' the sex boundary whenever I could, for fun. Don't get me wrong — my sexual feelings were always entirely female. I just enjoyed the independence I could suddenly have, when I changed roles." Helen paused. Averting her eyes from mine, she murmured, "But that created an unforeseen problem."

"Oh — what was that?"

Helen raised her eyes and looked me full in the face. A rosy flush suffused her features, reminding me of her reaction when I had teased her about the maid at Bavelaw.

"Oh Nick — can't you guess? I fell in love with you. Those long sessions teaching you to become a Scot at Hampton Court ... I tried to stop myself, knowing that it could lead to nothing — but it was no use. That's why I wouldn't join you to bring home the Summer on the Burgh Muir. I couldn't bear the thought of perhaps seeing you make advances to other girls."

My mind whirled. A dim realization of the pain I had unwittingly inflicted on Helen dawned on me. I recalled how I had light-heartedly boasted to Helen — 'Wattie' about conquests, how in her company I had ogled and flirted with girls during our time in Edinburgh, how I had slept in the same bed beside her, unaware of her real identity. All these must have been like knife-thrusts in her heart, each wound made all the keener because, trapped in her role of Wattie, she could allow no hint of her real feelings to surface. A tide of remorse mingled with a sudden rush of warm affection, surged through me.

"Oh Helen — I'm sorry," I muttered inadequately, shaking my head. I held out my arms and she flew into my embrace. Tentatively, I kissed her, then feeling her respond passionately, returned her kiss with fervour. Something stirred inside me — admiration for Helen's courage, integrity and professionalism; all that certainly, but something more besides. Here was a woman of rare quality I sensed, whose love was a pearl beyond price. I realized, with a pang of anguish for our predicament, that I was beginning to reciprocate Helen's feelings towards myself. Somehow, it felt as though we were made for each other, that her brave bright spirit was the lodestar for which my wandering yearnings had all along been searching. Even our backgrounds, though utterly contrasted geographically, were curiously similar, with their emphasis on business ventures undertaken on behalf of family interests. If only there were time, our relationship I knew would burgeon into something deep, stong and enduring. If only ... But the sand in the glass had almost run its course and soon the last grains must trickle away.

I murmured endearments to her, and saw with mingled awe and joy, her face turn radiant in the knowledge that her love was requited. I removed my own clothes, and spreading them with hers to cover the filth on the floor, made us a bed of sorts. We caressed each other's bodies, kindling a flame of desire, small at first, but as we fed it by degrees, burning strong and eager at last. We joined together in a kind of tender urgency, each aware of the other's desperate need...

Afterwards, as we lay at peace held close in each other's embrace, I thought that whatever terrible things Fate might have in store, they would somehow be bearable for we had between us created a kind of immortality.

We slept, then on waking continued to tell each other about ourselves. Helen went on to describe how a momentous trip to York (to settle a tangled matter of land-tenure referred from Durham to the Archbishop's Consistory Court) had changed the direction of her life. Here she had met Ascham, officially on sick-leave from Cambridge to recover from quartan fever, but actually engaged in work connected with the setting-up of the Court of Green Ginger. Based in Hull, Ascham had taken time off to come to York to help his ageing father sort out some family affairs, and had come across Helen Graham at the Consistory Court. Impressed by her intelligence, strength of personality and practical competence he had recognized her potential as an agent and had introduced himself to her. Conversation with Helen had confirmed his first impressions, and her ability to double as a man was an added recommendation. (Helen of course did not list her own qualities like this; I am 'reading between the lines' of her account, to express my own value-judgements concerning her character.)

Ascham had offered Helen a post as one of the 'Ladies of the Queen's Tiring Chamber' — an office especially created as a cover for the activities of a select handful of female agents. Her horsemanship, experience of handling weapons, ability to double as a man and to impersonate a Scot (being born and bred on the precise Frontier line had made her bi-lingual) made her a perfect choice for a field agent working in Scotland. The element of danger in the work had not deterred Helen, to whom violence and insecurity were daily facts of Border life, and the fact that she would have the opportunity of playing a man's role had been a powerful incentive. So she accepted.

151

Her family, ostensibly scornful of the fleshpots of the effete South, but secretly proud of the fact that 'our Helen' had been offered a position at Court, had not tried to block the apointment, and Helen had gone to London to begin training under the aegis of the Court of Green Ginger. Provided she didn't meet up with any close friends or relations who had known her as a woman, she was confident she could carry off the role.

"And how!" I broke in. "Your impersonation of a Scots hidalgo was masterly. I suppose Ascham sent you along with me to check that I didn't renege on the job."

"No Nick — I wasn't sent to keep tabs on you. Ascham thought highly of you, especially after that little showdown when Gardiner and Lamb pretended that I was going to be taken back to the Tower."

"The bastards," I breathed, half-admiringly, remembering the incident.

"Anyway — to explain my reason for accompanying you on the first stage of your mission," Helen went on. "Operation Porcupine had already cost Ascham two agents in the field. With time running out, he decided that two further agents working simultaneously but independently of each other would increase the chances of success."

"And of course, I didn't 'need to know' about your activities," I said with a smile, adding rather sourly, "though it doesn't seem to have applied the other way round; I suppose all organizations have a pecking order — sex descrimination I call it in this case. How did you make out, by the way?"

"So — so. After the Cauldstaneslap incident I returned to 'Uncle Andrew's' to 'regroup' as Ascham would say. By the way, the reason I tried to 'tough it out' with the gypsy leader was that I had important secret documents in my saddlebag. I'd picked them up from our Edinburgh depot — that's a private address where messages can be collected and delivered; the landlord asks no questions and pockets our fee. I was to deliver them to the Warden of the English Middle March who would send them on to Ascham. I didn't really think the gypsy would back down, but I felt I had to make the attempt.

"At that juncture, I was heading for Liddesdale to follow up my own private hunch that the Porcupine's den was in Hermitage Castle. But by the time I'd got back to Edinburgh and re-equipped myself, so much time had been lost that I decided to 'switch to Plan B'."

"'Plan B'?"

"We had a 'sleeper' in Musselburgh — planted there back in the '30's by Thomas Cromwell. Ascham had given me permission to 'wake' him if I got stuck. So I did just that. The sleeper reported that there had been a build-up of unusual activity centred on Fawside Castle east of Musselburgh. I decided to investigate; before doing so I wrote a sitrep for Ascham, which 'our man in Musselburgh' promised me would be in Wharton's hands within twenty-four hours. Following up the Fawside lead, I discovered that underground coal-workings at Dolphingston are being used as secret arsenals. Unfortunately, the Scots must have got on my scent; when I broke into Fawside Castle itself there was a reception committee waiting for me."

"Any evidence of the Porcupine?"

"No. But hazarding a guess, I'd say that the stockpiling of 'conventional' weapons in the Fawside area, could be an indication of preparations for a massive Scottish offensive; presumably the cutting edge would be provided by Porcupines. Now, tell me how you got on Nick."

I told Helen about my meeting with David Baxter in the leper-house, my gradual unravelling of his message, my sojourn with the gypsies (omitting my relations with Barbara), the clues I'd picked up at Lethington and the Abbey, my discovery of the conversion of doocots and mills to communications stations and components factories, and finally how my reputation as 'the lad wi the gowden preens' had led to my being summoned to Hailes as unwitting witch-finder. (The reason her arm hadn't bled when she stuck the pin in it, Helen explained, was because she had deliberately made the puncture where there was a mole.)

"Well done, Nick," Helen exclaimed softly when I had done. "We very nearly brought it off, didn't we? Pity no one's ever going to know." She lifted the wine bottle, in which a little still remained

153

and said with a smile, "To a gallant failure." She drank, then passed the bottle and I repeated the toast.

We discussed the implications of my discoveries and came to the following conclusions.

Ammunition — consisting of a charge of powder, or more likely powder plus shot, enclosed in a brass cartridge case, was being produced on a mass basis in stages at Lethington, St Mary's Abbey, and possibly the Gimmers Mills at Haddington. Gun barrels and other components were being manufactured at Preston Mill and perhaps at other mills, from steel produced in the Tranent-Gladsmuir area or imported via Aberlady. Hailes was the focal point and terminus for all this activity, being both ammunition depot, and plant where the components were assembled into the finished product — the Porcupine. (The hammering sounds issuing from the direction of the Chapel tended to reinforce this last supposition.)

The fact that the ammunition was being produced in such large quantities suggested that the cartridge cases must be expendable, which lent support to Ascham's theory that the Porcupine was a repeating weapon capable of sustained rapid fire.

So we had a general outline of the Porcupine project, but there were some gaps. Where did Markle fit into all of this? (Was it perhaps an Intelligence Headquarters?) What was the significance of the ignition-hole — if that was what it was, being at the rear of the cartridge? This seemed to imply that the Porcupine employed some revolutionary new system of ignition, in conjunction with some means of obtaining a gas-tight seal at the breech, as Ascham had postulated. As to the mechanical principles by which the Porcupine worked, we could not even guess.

For hours we continued talking, sharing confidences, re-capping on our adventures together as Jock and Wattie. (We laughed over the maid's failed seduction of Helen at Bavelaw, and the discovery of her sex by the gypsy women.) At length we dozed off into a fitful slumber.

I woke presently, aroused by a sound coming from outside the tower. Helen seemed to be fast asleep. Crossing the cell to the garderobe, I lay flat and peered through the circular opening. The hole commanded a view of part of a haugh, contained between the foot of the castle wall and the south bank of the Tyne.

The sound that had wakened me was caused by two men at work digging a hole. Presently, they put their mattocks down and moved away, outside my circle of vision, to return a few minutes later carrying a long heavy pole. They proceeded to set this upright in the hole, then they shovelled back soil round the sides and tamped it down firm. With a thrill of horror, I realized what the object was — the stake at which Helen was to be burned! This was shortly confirmed, when the men piled up bundles of faggots in a great cone round the base of the stake, first stapling on lengths of chain to secure the victim, then hammering in a long spike (to go between the victim's legs and support her weight, I supposed.) I resolved grimly, that Helen must not see the hideous apparatus for her execution, a glimpse of which would add mental torture to the physical anguish she must presently endure.

'MORTIS CUPIDITAS ...'

I WOKE to find the light of another dawn creeping into the pit. How was it possible, I wondered, to carry such a burden of foreboding and yet sleep? I could only suppose that once a certain threshold of stress had been reached, Nature provided her own anaesthetic.

Helen's eyes opened; a few seconds blankness, then terror registered, and an involuntary sob burst from her throat, as the terrible reality of her position crashed home, before she had time to muster her defences. I held her shaking body, while she fought for control.

"Sorry, Nick," she said at length, in a low but steady voice. "I'm all right now."

We looked into each other's eyes, seeing love and compassion reflected there. Then, without either of us saying anything, we both knew — I think at the same moment, what had to be done.

"Before they come for you," I whispered.

She nodded, a great relief and thankfulness that we had found this way, showing in her face. But first, we undressed and lay down together. Our lovemaking had a passionate tenderness that transcended anything I had known.

"I can go now with a quiet mind, my love," she said. Then she murmured to herself a haunting stanza, which is burned into my brain until the day when I too shall take my leave of life.

'Worm at my heart and fever in my head —
There is no peace for any but the dead.
Only the dead are beautiful and free —
Mortis cupiditas captavit me...'

"I'm ready, my love." Smiling, she knelt before me, lovely in her nakedness.

Tears coursed down my face as I wound her hose gently around her neck. My heart pounded and my hands shook so violently, that I doubted if they could accomplish their task. Then from

156

somewhere inside me strength welled up, calming the tumult in my breast, steadying my hands.

I pulled … She struggled briefly; then death came, swift and easy.

When I had wept my grief out, I laid her body down tenderly, then dressed, feeling nothing except an aching emptiness. Presently, the hatch grated open and the gaoler called, "Come, witch."

The events that followed seemed like a dream sequence — the gaoler's consternation when he discovered the truth, guards milling about above the hatch, shouted orders, my removal from the pit, being marched under escort to the trial chamber …

Patrick Hepburn, his face red with fury, burst through the door. "This is yeir fault," he roared at the unfortunate gaoler. "Whit fur did ye no keep better gyaird?"

"How wis Ah tae ken, Yeir Grace?" protested the wretched man, cowering away from Hepburn's menacing bulk.

"Haud yeir wheesht, ye feckless gomeril," snarled Hepburn, sending the gaoler reeling with a savage back-handed blow.

Mastering his fury with an obvious effort, he turned to myself. "So — ye wad cheat the law," he said, in ominously quiet tones.

I shrugged. "Your Grace knows the saying — 'all's fair in love and war'."

Madness burned in Hepburn's eyes and for a moment I thought that he would strike me. Then his expression changed, and he laughed aloud.

"Touché!" he exclaimed. "By Christ, but ye're a cool yin. Tae turn the tables on Patrick Hepburn — there's no mony can say they've done thon." He looked at me appraisingly. "Thon offer Ah made ye — it still stands."

For a moment, I was sorely tempted. Then a hot flush of shame swept over me. To agree would be to put Helen's sacrifice at nought, to send Mossman to the gallows or worse, to betray my country. I shook my head.

"So be it," said Hepburn. "Ah'll need tae send a signed Confession tae Arran. It's yeir privilege tae hae a trial furst, gin that's yeir wish." He smiled wryly. "But we'll no insist on it."

"Thanks — but no."

My confession had already been made out. I signed it, and was being escorted out, when a sudden fancy made me turn at the door.

"Any chance of a last request being granted, Your Grace?" A day earlier I would have tempered valour with discretion; now I had ceased to care.

Hepburn looked at me quizzically. "Try me."

"I don't suppose you'd let me in on — 'Scotland's Muckle Secret' I think you called it."

Hepburn stared at me, then slapping his thigh, gave a shout of laughter.

"Hear that, lads," he exlaimed to the two guards. "He wants fur tae ken wur Muckle Secret. Ye're a caution, quacksalver. Man, Ah like ye. A peety ye werena born a Scot. Ach, Ah dinna ken fur why ye shouldna see it. Bide ye here an keek oot the windae, when ye hear the sodgers ootside." And he departed, after assigning one of the guards to stay behind with me.

Presently, food was sent — mutton pies and a flagon of wine. I fell to, inviting the guard to help himself from the flagon.

"No fur me pal — but thanks a the same," replied the guard, a blue-chinned old sweat, with a hint of humour about the eyes and mouth.

"What did His Grace mean by telling me to look out of the window when I heard the soldiers?" I asked.

"They riders o Hertfords whit wis tane — they've telt us a they ken, which wisna verra muckle. Noo, we'll gie them a risp o 'the Earl o Bothwell's Tirlin Pin'." He cleared his throat and studiedly looked at the ceiling. "Forbye twa that's tae witness the execution the morn." Tactfully switching the subject, he said, "Man — Ah heard tell how ye gied yon gyler his comeuppance. Guid on ye lad. There's nane o us gyairds has ony time fur thon black-avised skellum."

"'The Earl of Bothwell's Tirling Pin'?"

"There they're comin the noo. Keek oot the windae an ye'll see whit Ah mean. Me — Ah'll no bother; Ah've seen it a afore."

I walked to the tall barred window and looked out. A little procession was issuing through the watergate just to the east of my pit prison, and filing onto the haugh by the river — four bound

158

prisoners and six guards. They were followed a few moments later by two men carrying a long box, suspended between them by means of rope handles. I had thought myself drained empty of emotion, but as I watched, I felt my heart begin to pound within my breast. The box, I knew, contained the Porcupine.

THE EARL OF BOTHWELL'S
TIRLING PIN

THE LAST to emerge from the watergate was a tall man, dressed in black, with fine aquiline features and hair unfashionably long. He stalked over to the pair who had been carrying the box, which they had now set down. Twenty yards in front, close to the stake, the prisoners had been halted by their escort. The tranquil setting, bathed in sunlight, seemed to point up the grimness of the little drama about to unfold.

"Who's the fellow in black with the long hair?" I asked the guard.

"Thon'll be Signor Benvenuto — Black Ben we cries him. An Eytie boffin; he's the heid bummer o the hale jing-bang. Some fowk say he's a natural son o a Mister da — whit-dae-ye-macry-it? Vinci. Aye da Vinci, thon wis fut."

Completely fascinated now, I watched as, under the eagle eye of Black Ben, the two men lifted a folding tripod from the box. Next came a bizarre-looking object consisting of the following: first a bundle of gun barrels exactly resembling the 'fasces' carried by Roman lictors; behind this bundle and encasing it at the breech end, massive steel housing, with an aperture at the top revealing a heavy steel cylinder with multiple tiny perforations, positioned behind the gun barrels; a brass-handled lever at the rear of the housing, and below the lever a crank-handle.*

This unit — barrels, housing and breech mechanism, was now bolted onto a steel or wrought-iron mounting or 'cradle' with a rod at the bottom. The whole was now lifted up, and the rod inserted into a cylindrical steel casing at the centre of the tripod, thus allowing the gun to swivel. (The central arm of the cradle was adjustable, to permit the piece to be elevated or depressed.)

One of the gun-crew now lifted from the box a plate with multiple perforations, from which projected a bunch of brass cylinders — identical to the one I had picked up near Lethington.

See Wainwright's Drawing. (Transcriber)

His companion pulled the lever, and the steel cylinder behind the barrels slid back, allowing the plate holding the charges (for the brass cylinders could be nothing else) to be dropped into position behind the barrels. The lever was now pushed forward, thrusting home the cylindrical breech-block which thus chambered the cartridges into the barrels.

One of the crew crouched behind the Porcupine, the other standing by with a second plate of cartridges. A tense silence spread throughout the assembly. Black Ben raised his hand.

The guards, who had untied their captives and were holding them by the arms, now released them, and dashed back behind the gun-crew to watch the fun. The prisoners began to sprint for their lives along the haugh, in the opposite direction. Black Ben's hand swept down ...

The crank handle began to revolve, and immediately a stuttering roar broke out. Orange flashes leapt from the gun barrels in turn. Dust-puffs spurted round the fugitives' heels. Two of them stumbled and pitched forward on their faces, to lie twitching on the sward. The remaining two began to jink and weave, in a desperate bid to elude the stream of bullets. Remorselessly, the Porcupine tracked them with a swinging scythe of lead. One checked in mid-stride with a scream, somersaulted in the air and crashed to the ground, where he lay still. The other managed to reach the river bank and flung himself into the Tyne.

The clattering din cut out abruptly. The ensuing silence was like a thunderclap. Frenetic activity round the Porcupine ... lever swung back ... plate with expended cartridges withdrawn ... fresh plate inserted ... lever shoved forward ...

The swimmer reached the far side and began to scramble up the bank. Then the obscene tattoo rattled out once more. A line of fountains raced across the Tyne. The man gave a choked cry and flung up his hands. He tumbled back into the river with a splash, then slid below the surface.

Transcription of the legend accompany Wainwright's drawing of the Porcupine.

To thintente that I would showe my goodewill to make all thinges as easy to the sense of the reader as my knowledge could instruct: I have devised and drawne accordynge to my cunnynge a likenesse of the Porpentyne (that the Scottes name the Erle of Bothwelles Tirling Pinne) suche as in my memorie I could since calle to mynd. Noe exquisite observaunce of gemoetricall dimension but yet neither soe grosse nor far from the truth I trust but that hit may serve for some ease of understandynge.

The Porpentyne

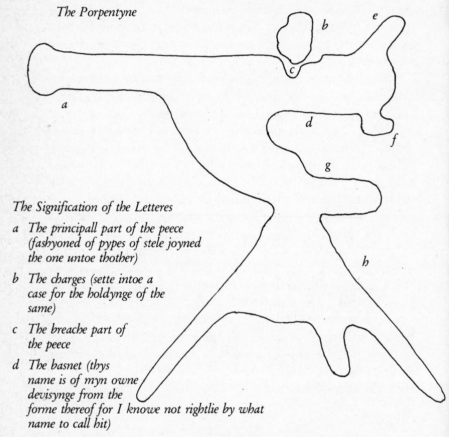

The Signification of the Letteres

a   The principall part of the peece
    (fashyoned of pypes of stele joyned
    the one untoe thother)

b   The charges (sette intoe a
    case for the holdynge of the
    same)

c   The breache part of
    the peece

d   The basnet (thys
    name is of myn owne
    devisynge from the
    forme thereof for I knowe not rightlie by what
    name to call hit)

e   For the drawinge in and movinge forthe of the breeche part

f   On beeinge turned around it causeth an engyne to stryke the charges

g   The cradle

h   The tripos

To thintente that I would shewe my goodewill to make all thinges as easie
to the sense of y reader as my knowledge could instruct: I have devised and
drawne accordynge to my cunnynge a likenesse of y Perpentyne (y y
Scottt name the tale of Bothwelles tirling Pinne) suche as in my
memorie I could imre.... to mynd. Not the quisite observaunce of geometric-
all dimension but yet neither soo grosse nor farr fro y truth I trust but that
hit may serve for some ease of understandynge.

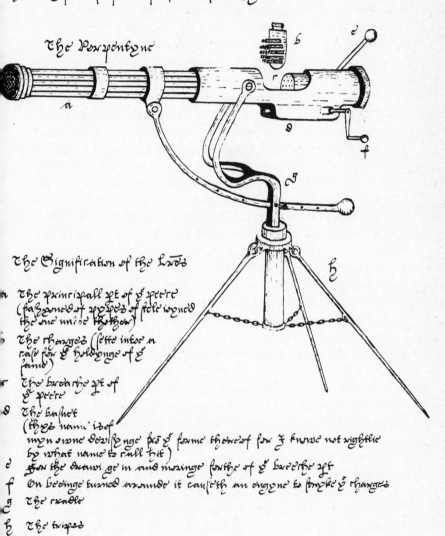

The Perpentyne

The Signification of the Lres

a The principall pt of y peece
  (fashioned of ropes of stele ioyned
  the one unto thother)

b The chardges (sette intoo a
  case for y holdynge of y
  same)

c The breathe pt of
  y peece

d The basket
  (this name is of
  myn owne devisynge fro y forme thereof for I knowe not rightlie
  by what name to call hit)

e For the drawynge in and movinge forthe of y breathe pt

f On beeinge turned arounde it causeth an engyne to stryke y chardges

g The cradle

h The tripes

Back in the pit prison (from which they'd removed Helen's body), I mulled over the events I had just witnessed. Ascham's theory about what had happened at Ancrum Moor had been inspired deduction, the Porcupine's performance exactly matching his imagined reconstruction of sustained fire from a repeating firearm. Used properly, i.e. as infantry weapons, not as artillery pieces which could be located and knocked out by cannon fire, Porcupines would make a Scottish army irresistible. Here was the successor to the barrage of clothyard shafts which had proved the death-knell of the armoured knight, and whose passing Ascham so bitterly lamented — but a successor a hundred-fold more deadly. Firing from prepared positions, Porcupines would simply mow down troops advancing in their path. And they were sufficiently light, and capable of rapid enough assembly, to be mobile; a Porcupine plus its ammunition could easily be carried by a single mule. Thus it could be used in a fluid tactical situation, both in an offensive and a defensive role.

I considered the wider implications and found them chilling. (My own predicament seemed for the moment to dwindle into insignificance by comparison.) Would the Scots rest content with a policy of merely keeping the Auld Enemy at bay? Hardly. An offensive would be mounted; if the Scots's allies the French got the Porcupine, that would spell certain defeat for England. But suppose it didn't stop there? Suppose France's Turkish allies were to acquire the weapon? Or worse still, the totalitarian Russia of Ivan the Terrible? The consequences for European civilization could be catastrophic, I thought, recalling the conversation between Ascham and myself at our first meeting. Ivan would roll back his enemies the Swedes and the Poles in the west and gain his 'window on the Baltic' to match his policy of eastern expansion. Would he stop there? There was no reason to suppose he would. However one looked at it, the future seemed bleak — an escalating 'arms race' or the destruction of Western civilization by Eastern hordes.

How did the Porcupine work? I wondered. There was no external lock mechanism to ignite the charges — therefore they must be ignited internally. But how? It seemed to me a technical impossibility. The other two problems inherent in making a repeating weapon capable of sustained fire, which Ascham had

164

outlined — namely prepared expendable cartridges, and a gas-tight seal at the breech, had been brilliantly solved, as I had just seen. I recalled that the cartridge case I had picked up had had a projecting rim at the base. This would hold it secure in the carrying plate, which would be rammed up snug against the breech end of the barrels (the cartridges themselves being pushed into the barrels), when the heavy breech-block was levered home, thus creating a most efficient seal. Also — the cartridge cases, being of soft brass, would (unlike the iron cartridge cases for the carbine I'd practised with at Hampton Court) expand when fired, thus increasing their self-obturating qualities. Individual gunsmiths had already come very close to solving some of the problems which the construction of an efficient repeating weapon posed. Now, an obscure Italian genius, by combining this knowledge with his own developments — a gas-tight seal at the breech, and a system of internal ignition, had 'broken through' these technical barriers and at last created such a weapon. Martin Luther has said, 'Firearms are the direct suggestion of the Devil.' If for 'Firearm' one reads 'Porcupine', I am tempted to believe he might have been right.

THE THIGHBONE AND THE RING

I JERKED AWAKE from a doze. What had roused me? There it was — a chinking noise. I crawled over to the garderobe, and lying down, looked through the hole. The haugh was dotted with roughly-made tents, among which moved dogs and dark-complexioned folk, dressed in garish clothing — a gypsy encampment. They must have just arrived, as some tents were still being pitched, and not all the baggage animals had been unburdened. Nevertheless, some gypsies had already collected pots and pans from the castle kitchen and were mending them.

I wondered why Patrick Hepburn hadn't moved them on. Normally, gypsies would have been welcome visitors at a great establishment, for their skill in carrying out running repairs to kitchen utensils. For reasons of security however, the last thing Bothwell needed I would have thought, was the presence of a bunch of thievish and inquisitive vagrants. Then I saw that this was yet another instance of Hepburn's cunning. (The guards and artisans in the castle were presumably hand-picked for being close-mouthed, and could be trusted not to gossip.) Anyone hearing that the gypsies had encamped at Hailes would assume that Hepburn had nothing to hide. If however, he was known to have chased them away ...

As I gazed at the encampment, I remembered my time with Barbara and a wave of poignant longing swept over me, for love, for the open air, for freedom. Then I remembered her parting words as she slipped her ring onto my finger; 'gin ye ever need help, show this tae a Faa an they'll ken ye fur Jock Trummle whae cured their Queen.'

With the memory, a wild excitement surged through me, as hope, which had been dead, revived again. I slipped off the ring (which Hepburn's guards — a hard lot but not common thieves, had let me keep, along with Jessie's pendant). Then my excitement died down a bit as practical problems occurred to me — how was I going to show the ring? suppose they were Baillies, not Faas?

The temptation to yell through the garderobe was almost overwhelming, but I fought it down. That would be to invite disaster; I could imagine a crowd collecting, guards arriving to see what the brouhaha was about ... I must be patient, circumspect.

Assess, plan, act. Rootling among the filth on the floor, I rescued the longest chicken bones from our meal of the previous day. From the shadow cast by the stake, I judged it to be around midday. I settled down beside the garderobe to wait.

As the shadow of the stake slowly lengthened, my frustration and impatience gave way to something close to despair. Once, a woman headed in my direction, and I hurled one of my stock of bones, only to see it pounced on by a dog and borne away. On a second occasion, my missile fell short, and the gypsy passed without noticing.

Darkness flowed across the bottom of the pit. Outside, the cooking fires were being lit; soon the gypsies would be in their tents for the night. To have allowed myself to hope again, then to have that hope shrivel and die, was almost beyond bearing. Suddenly I tensed, as I spotted a tall figure circling the encampment at a leisurely pace — one of their leaders doing the rounds, making sure that all was well for the night probably.

I waited in an agony of expectation, as the man, in the course of his circuit, gradually approached the garderobe exit. If he held to his course, he would pass it at a distance of some ten yards.

I picked up a thigh bone in trembling fingers, willing myself not to throw it prematurely. The man stopped beside a tent and chatted for an interminable time while my nerves stretched to breaking point. He was moving again, stopping to scan the sky, moving once more, coming level with the garderobe ... *Now*!

I drew back my hand and pitched the bone through the hole. It hit the grassy slope, bounced once, and rolled to a halt in front of the gypsy. For a terrible moment, I thought he hadn't seen it. But he stopped beside the bone; instead of picking it up, he stood tense and listening, like a pointer on the alert.

"Koshto divvus (Hallo there)," I called softly in Romany, a few phrases of which I had picked up from Barbara.

167

The man, showing no sign that he had heard me, sauntered over to the garderobe, and ignoring the filth that crusted the exit, put his face close to the hole — a saturnine, cunning face with a hint of authority to the set of the jaw. He rattled off something under his breath in the tinkler speech.

"I'm a gorgio (non-gypsy)," I said. "My name's Jock Trummle."

The man blinked, clearly surprised. Then the brooding mask was slipped on again.

"Gie's a sign," he murmured.

I rolled the ring down the pipe; he caught it, and after a brief examination, flicked it deftly back.

"So ye're the lad whit cured wur Queen. Her lot's awa doon past Cockburnspath. Whit can Ah dae fur ye, Jock Trummle?" It may have been imagination, but I thought I detected a note of warmth in the man's voice which had not been there before.

"There's a trapdoor in the roof of this cell I'm in," I said. "If you can get inside the castle and open it, then let down the rope. Watch out for the gaol —"

My voice trailed away; the man was already continuing his round. Had he dismissed my request out of hand as being too difficult and dangerous? As I knew from experience, once they had accepted you, there were no more generous and loyal people on earth than the gypsies. And if anyone could fabricate an excuse to get inside the castle and snoop around without being noticed, that person was a gypsy. But there were limits to what you could reasonably expect of them; I began to think that I had overstepped those limits.

The pit filled with darkness. The noises from the gypsy encampment — clash of dishes, soft laughter, dogs yapping, stilled one by one. Above me, I could hear faint callings as the guard was changed. Once the gaoler came to gloat. "Dinna fash yeirsel, gin ye feel cauld in the nicht," he called through the grille. "Come the morn, ye'll get a richt warmin." And he moved off, chuckling at his tasteless joke.

The hours bled slowly away. Hope had sunk to a flickering ember, when I heard a faint scrape above me. My heart thumping wildly, I scrambled to my feet and moved under the hatch. Looking up, I could just make out a dim shape silhouetted in the opening.

Something brushed past me and thumped softly on the floor. The rope!

I slipped a foot into the loop at the end of the rope, and tugged to show that I was ready. I found myself rising ... I braced a hand and knee on the edge of the opening and clambered out of the pit. I tried to locate my rescuer, to extend some sign of thanks. But the man had gone.

THE PORCUPINE'S LAIR

AS I STOOD in the darkness, trying to orientate myself, I became aware of the sound of distant but approaching footsteps. Had the gaoler heard something? The entrance to the chamber I was in gradually materialized as a pale rectangle. I shrank against the wall, hoping that whoever was bearing the light, would prove to be a guard on his rounds and pass by.

A figure bearing a lantern entered the chamber — the gaoler. Spotting the open hatchway, he uttered a curse and hurried towards it. As he passed me, I let him have the full Martin treatment — my foot lashed upwards, slamming into the underside of his jaw. There was a crackle of breaking bone; dropping the lantern, the man collapsed without a sound. I dragged his inert body to the open hatch and pushed him over the edge; he struck the floor with a heavy thump. I lowered the iron grille and shot the bolt.

Dowsing the lantern, I descended a short flight of stairs to a passage which I remembered led to the courtyard. A few seconds later I was in the open air; as my eyes became accustomed to the gloom, I made out above me the loom of the West Tower which I had just quitted, and on the far side of the courtyard, the curtain wall, black against a starlit sky.

Now what? Fighting down an animal instinct to cut and run, I repeated Ascham's formula to myself, 'Assess, plan, act.' I cursed myself for not finishing off the gaoler while I had the chance; too late now. But with luck, he would be unconscious for some time yet. Long enough for me to locate the Porcupine and destroy it? Don't think of time running out, concentrate on each step as it comes. The chapel — that was my most likely target.

I crept stealthily into the courtyard, and looked around, listening. Apart from the measured pacing of a guard on the curtain walk, I could hear nothing. Seemingly, the castle had shut down for the night, except in one place; light streamed through the windows of the long building between the two towers — the chapel.

I moved up to the chapel and examined the wall. Diffused light from the windows enabled me to make out a projecting block — almost like a corbel, below the easternmost of the two windows. Using this as a handhold, I was able to get enough purchase on the rough ashlar of the wall to haul myself up and peep through the window.

This is what I saw: long tables, littered with components and tools, and on which, in various stages of assembly, were four Porcupines; along the walls in racks and bundles, military stores — hackbuts, bowstaves, bowstrings, spears, sheaves of arrows .. ; seated at a desk with his back to me, by the light of the torches flaring in wall-sconces, a man writing — Signor Benvenuto, by his long hair and black clothing.

I descended to the ground, then mounted the wooden staircase leading to the chapel doorway. Breathing deeply to get my racing pulse and thumping heart under control, I tried the handle. It turned; I pushed and the door gave. With infinite caution, I continued to push and the door swung back, mercifully without a creak. I slipped through the gap. On a peg in the wall behind him, hung Benvenuto's cloak and sword belt. Thanking God for Martin's training, which had never stood me in better stead than now, I reached the hanging articles in two long catlike strides, before the seated man was aware of my presence. Too late, he turned his head, his eyes widening; before he had time to react and raise the alarm, I had plucked the dagger from its sheath and was holding the point under his chin, while my other hand clapped itself over his mouth.

"One cry for help ... ," I whispered, and pressed the dagger to reinforce the hint; a drop of blood welled from the tiny puncture. Benvenuto nodded — as far as was possible below my restraining hand. Cautiously, I released my grip.

I indicated the partly-assembled Porcupines on the tables. "How many of these are completed?"

Benvenuto looked at me — sad luminous eyes in a fine face, a strong yet sensitive face. If Leonardo had ever fathered a son, it would not be difficult to believe that this man could be he.

"As we have not been introduced Signor," replied Benvenuto in a

171

softly Italian accent, "forgive me if I assume for the present, that you are an enemy agent." Despite a slight tremor in his voice, he had control of himself, and managed to preserve an aura of calm dignity. "I shall answer 'yes' or 'no' to your questions. Thus much is permissible under duress, I think. Anything else — you will have to discover for yourself."

I decided that strong-arm tactics would be unproductive with this man. "Fair enough. The completed weapons are stored in this room?"

"That is so."

"And this other stuff — part of an arms cache in preparation for an invasion of England?"

"Si — I believe so."

"When?"

Benvenuto shook his head. "Remember the rules we agreed on, my friend," he said with a grave smile. "'Yes' or 'no'."

After several minutes of intensive questioning I had elicited the following information: around forty Porcupines had been manufactured to date and were stored in the chapel; there were several other arms caches, for example the ones in the Fawside Castle area, but of 'conventional' weapons only, located at various points in the Lowlands; Porcupines had indeed been responsible for the English rout at Ancrum Moor. Further questioning was interrupted by a sudden uproar outside in the courtyard; the gaoler must have managed to raise the alarm, or been discovered.

I ducked under the desk, fighting panic. "This dagger's going to be pointing at your guts," I told Benvenuto. "Co-operate, and you'll be okay. Try any tricks, and you get it — that's a promise."

I heard the door crash open. "'scuse us burstin in on ye Signor Benvenuto Sur," a voice called. "There's a dangerous prisoner escapit. Jist makin sure he wisna in here, Sur."

"As you see — there is only myself," I heard Benvenuto reply, I went limp with relief.

"Okay then Sur. Mind an keep the door lockit; he's a desperate chiel whae'll stap at naethin. Sorry fur disturbin ye Sur."

The door shut and I emerged. "Well done," I said. "That was fine. We'd best do as the man said — you have a key?"

"It is in the lock."

I felt considerably less vulnerable when I had turned the key. Then, as I returned to Benvenuto, a grim realization dawned upon me. I might succeed in destroying the Porcupines, but that in itself would achieve little unless I also destroyed their creator.

Either this must have shown in my face, or Benvenuto had made the same deduction, for he suddenly went pale and fought to control the trembling that had seized his body.

"I realize what you have to do," he said hoarsely. "I shall not resist. What would be the use? I am not — how do you say, a 'man of action'. I only carry weapons as a badge of rank. A scholar, a scientist — that is Benvenuto."

I had no wish to prolong the man's agony of mind, but I could not help myself asking, "What stopped you from warning the guard? Even if you hadn't realized then that you'd nothing to lose, you'd have saved the secret weapon."

"My friend, my own life and the fate of 'the Earl of Bothwell's Tirling Pin' as they call it, are things that no longer concern me greatly. When he was in Venice, I met the Earl of Bothwell and became his friend, as I thought. Among other things, I spoke of my research and achievements in the field of engineering and military science. It was I who organized the defence works of Rimini against the Turks. As Bothwell's friend, I came to Hailes when he invited me, little suspecting that I was walking into a cage. Oh, the bars are gilded — I am treated with respect, honour even, shown every consideration. But for all that, I am a prisoner. I am confined to Hailes, and must work to develop their secret engine of war."

Benvenuto looked at me with a sort of weary resignation. "I have succeeded — but I feel no pride in the achievement. Life has become a bitter, empty thing. My creation sickens me; I think with horror of the death and chaos it will unloose. I am forced to preside over executions — of 'traitors and criminals' they are careful to inform me, and I have witnessed its terrible power. Destroy it with my blessing." A beseeching note crept into his voice. "Perhaps my friend — if I were to promse that I would never begin the work again ... "

"But you can't make such a promise," I said. "We both know

173

they would be too strong for you."

Benvenuto began to shake violently, hearing his death-sentence in my words. God — if only there were another way. But there wasn't; steeling myself, I drove the dagger home ...

Benvenuto stiffened and gasped. His eyes widened, registered surprise, then — nothing.

Hating myself, hating Ascham and the whole foul business that had forced me to kill in cold blood, a good and innocent man, I arranged the body, and put a pen between the lifeless fingers, so that to a casual glance it looked as though Benvenuto were working at the desk. Dashing hot tears from my eyes, I experienced a wave of disillusionment and self-disgust. Is this what spying did to you — destroyed you from within, if you survived long enough? Helen, who had been longer in the game than myself, had felt its corrupting touch:

'Worm at my heart and fever in my head —
There is no peace for any but the dead ...'
Would I ever be clean again?

With a huge effort, I put everything else out of my mind and forced myself to concentrate on the task in hand. I found the Porcupines which had been completely assembled easily enough. They were stacked in the corner nearest the doorway, contained in long crates covered by tarpaulins. With a jemmy from a work bench I prised one open — the weapon inside was identical to the one I had seen in action that afternoon, the parts heavily greased against rusting. Another tarpaulin-covered mound consisted of square crates, whose contents proved to be the now-familiar brass cartridges — heaped in glittering profusion like some goblin treasure hoard. I stuffed a handful into a pocket of my tunic. In a piscina opposite the doorway, I found stacked several smallish kegs which, after I had drawn the bung from one, I discovered contained gunpowder.

I proceeded to construct a gigantic bonfire — powder kegs forming the foundation, then the Porcupines in their crates plus the partly-assembled ones on the work-benches, ammunition next, finally armfuls of spears, bows, hackbuts. Suddenly, I remembered something — perhaps the most important item of all. Returning to the desk, I examined the litter of papers in front of Benvenuto's cooling corpse. Here were the plans of the Porcupine — beautifully-executed and detailed, showing the components separately, also assembled. I hesitated; this knowledge would ensure England's military supremacy for decades to come. But suppose I were caught with the plans on me? The Porcupine, like the Phoenix, would rise again from the ashes. Then the words of Martin Luther flashed again into my brain, and I hesitated no longer but added the mass of papers to the pyre; for the knowledge they contained was evil.

Holding the keg I had opened to my chest, with both arms, I proceeded to lay a powder trail from the great mound of armaments, round the walls of the chapel, to end at a point near the door, so that I could ignite it as I left. The train laid, I buckled on Benvenuto's sword-belt and donned the cloak, pulling the hood up over my head. With a modicum of luck, this disguise should be proof against any casual encounter, especially at night.

I was about to take a torch from the wall in order to fire the train, when I realized that the sounds of the search, which I had dimly been aware of as a background of shouts and running footsteps, had stopped, to be replaced by a swelling murmur from the direction of the Tyne. I moved across to one of the windows in the north wall of the chapel and, taking care to avoid showing my silhouette, looked down upon the haugh.

DESTRUCTION BY FIRE

AN EXPECTANT CROWD made up of the inhabitants of the castle and castleton, plus the gypsies, was milling about around the stake. Then a hush spread throughout the throng, as a figure was led through the watergate. Though I could not recognize him, for he was stripped to his shirt and hose, and his head was enclosed in that hideous contraption the witch's bridle, I guessed that the prisoner could only be the gaoler.

Here was poetic justice with a vengeance! I could only imagine that Hepburn, mad with rage at my escape (from the castle, he must assume, the search for me having proved fruitless), had resolved to make an object-lesson of the wretched gaoler. No doubt he held the man responsible for my escape, and also wanted the two remaining prisoners to witness what happened to English spies; (they weren't to know of course that the gaoler was a substitute). The timing, which was inappropriate to say the least, was some indication of the blind violence of Bothwell's fury.

I watched in horrified fascination, as the struggling wretch was dragged to the stake and lifted up to straddle the spike, so that it projected between his legs like an obscene phallus. The chains were then wrapped round him and secured with padlocks.

A great sigh rose from the crowd, as a guard came forward with a flaming torch. The man set the torch to the brushwood below the faggots.

The warm dry weather had made the pyre like tinder. The brushwood blazed up with a hungry crackle, and smoke spurted from the faggots. Red tongues flickered among the logs, then with a whooshing roar the pyre burst into flames. The chained victim began to writhe, and terrible sounds issued from behind the bridle. His hose, shirt and hair flared briefly then were gone, and a tide of blisters rippled up his body below the shrivelling skin. The flames licked higher; spike, chains and bridle glowed dull orange and the twisting flesh began to blacken. Then, mercifully, a great column of fire leapt up to engulf him, cutting short his agony.

Sickened and appalled, I turned away. Grabbing a torch from a sconce, I touched off the train, hurled myself through the doorway and sprinted down the staircase ...

I had nearly reached the watergate when an ear-splitting detonation sounded from above me and the cobbles leapt beneath my feet. I burst onto the haugh.

The execution of the gaoler was now eclipsed by an even more arresting spectacle; the crowd stared at an incredible fireworks display taking place above their heads. A series of deafening bangs ripped out as the powder-kegs exploded with blinding flashes, bathing the haugh in flickers of momentary daylight. A fountain of flame and debris spewed up through the chapel roof. With a sound like giants shaking titanic rattles, the ammunition began to explode, the poppings blending at last into a continous crackling roar, while bullets zipped and shrieked like nightmare hornets.

Suddenly, a stentorian bellow cut through the din; "Dinna jist stan there — fetch water!"

Bothwell's order broke the spell. The crowd disintegrated as its members hastened to obey. Time to go. Amid the hurry and confusion, no one paid me the slightest attention as I slipped away in the shadow of the West Tower. I headed upstream along the Tyne for two or three hundred yards, wading in the shallows at the water's edge, to break my trail should bloodhounds be used to track me. Then turning to my left at a right angle to the river, I crossed the road and headed in a bee-line for Dunpender Law ...

From my sanctuary, I watched the inferno in Hailes Castle gradually brought under control. Dawn showed a few wisps of smoke still rising from the chapel, which from this distance looked to be a burnt-out shell. It also showed a line of figures issuing from the castle, signifying that the hunt for myself was under way again.

THE QUILL OF THE PORCUPINE

FOR FIVE DAYS I lay low in my Pictish earth-house, subsisting on my store of salted flesh, only emerging at night for purposes of nature, to replenish my water-supply, and to gather fresh bracken. (It was necessary to change the camouflage concealing the bunker's opening fairly frequently, as dried-up bracken would have been a dead give-away.)

Though by day I could see Hepburn's patrols, supplemented by local tenantry, beating the surrounding countryside with assiduous thoroughness, I was at no time in danger of being discovered, except once — when a search party passed within twenty yards of my hiding-place.

I had plenty of time to give myself a thorough 'de-briefing', as Ascham would have put it, concerning Operation Porcupine. I had little doubt that my holocaust in the chapel had been the end of the Porcupine. Physically, all that could remain would be some twisted lumps of metal. Without Benvenuto and the plans, the Scots would never re-create it. I had slain the monster, and in so doing had perhaps wrought a great service to mankind, yet the taste of victory was as dust and ashes in the mouth. I was young, I told myself, the human mind and body are resilient and I would become whole again. But I knew that I would carry some of the scars of the business to my grave. One thing was sure — never again would I turn my hand to this game of spying, not even were Ascham to offer me a Dukedom and all the gold of Ophir.

I examined the cartridges I had taken from the crate of ammunition, and made the following discovery. In the base of each, where the perforation in the original case I'd picked up was, a flattened plug of some soft metal had been inserted. How to open it? Apart from my dwindling stock of provisions, my map and the water pitcher, my only possessions were what I stood up in. (Benvenuto's cloak and sword-belt, I had weighted with a stone and dumped in the Tyne, in the course of my flight from the castle.) But on the floor of my shelter, I found one of those shaped flint points called elf-bolts, but which I suspect were made by men in a past age before the Flood — for this one's shape was exactly that of a modern arrow-head. With it, by dint of patient boring, I was able to perforate the metal plug, when some greyish powder trickled out onto my palm.

This grey substance (which in colour and texture no way resembled gunpowder), formed, I suspected, the priming for the charge. But how — if it was sealed up in a metal capsule, could it be ignited? Would it perhaps explode if you hit it? I searched until I found two flat 'chuckie-stanes', as the Scots call smooth pebbles. Placing one on the floor, I poured the grey powder onto its face, and carefully placed the other pebble on top. Removing my shoe, I held it by the toe, and whacked it down on the upper pebble. There was a flash, accompanied by a sharp report, and the topmost stone flew in smithereens.

So that was the final secret of the Porcupine! The charge was set off by a capsule, containing a substance which exploded by *percussion* — thus obviating the need for external ignition. I recalled that the heavy breech block had contained tiny multiple perforations. These perforations must be to allow the passage of thin rods — or rather, thick needles. In my mind's eye, the missing pieces of the mosaic were falling into place, almost more quickly than my brain could interpret their significance. Each perforation would be in line with one of the Porcupine's barrels. Rotating the crank-handle must operate some device (possibly a spring-loaded mechanism), which would drive each needle in turn along its hole in the breech-block, to strike the explosive capsule set in the base of the cartridge. This would then detonate, igniting the charge inside the cartridge case. I recalled the scene in Preston Mill; in addition to gun barrels, there had been squat steel cylinders with multiple perforations. I hadn't known what they were then — now I realized that they were breech-blocks for the Porcupine. Were the capsules to detonate the main charge, manufactured in Markle? I wondered. It was possible — the skills, knowledge and precision needed to make and handle the dangerously volatile grey powder, would be consistent with a monastic establishment.

179

I picked out the wadding at the other end of the cartridge, and found as I expected, a conventional bullet and powder charge behind it.

I reflected on the reason which had brought about the Porcupine's creation — a small nation, driven by one larger and more powerful, to seek desperate measures for its own survival.

* *In view of the possible 'Leonardo Connection,' it is perhaps a little disappointing that the cartridge did not contain a modern-style conical bullet — In addition to designing projectiles detonated by percussion, Leonardo drew streamlined shells exactly resembling those in use today.* (Transcriber)

THE HAUGHS OF LEADER

ON THE FIFTH DAY of my vigil in the bunker, I saw that activity from Hailes had become perfunctory and sporadic. I decided accordingly, to make my break that night. I would try to contact the second on my list of 'safe houses' — Auldbiggin near Lauder.

When the last lights of Hailes — both Castle and township, were extinguished, I crept from my den, my remaining provisions and my map stuffed in my tunic. The cartridges I left behind, to keep company with the flint arrowhead; perhaps in some distant age, someone will find them and wonder what they are.

It was a fine clear night with a sickle moon and a powdering of stars, to make my progress easy. Locating the Pole Star from the Plough, I got my bearings and struck out south-west into the Lammermuir foothills. Bypassing the hamlet of Morham, I reached the Hopes Water above Yester in something between two and three hours, I reckoned. I followed the Hopes valley to its head, and climbing out of the glen, picked up my old friend the track which I had travelled with the Faas — a thousand years ago, it seemed. There was the great whaleback of the Lammer Law, looming against the sky to my right, so I must have intersected the track at almost the exact spot where we had fought the Baillies.

I headed south along the track, for I knew Lauderdale to be the next valley in that direction, and sure enough, as dawn was breaking, I came down off the hill into a strath which I thought could only be the Haughs of Leader. Following the river for a mile, I came to a confluence with a stream, coming in from the north. I repeated the address to myself; 'Auldbiggin, a farm town with policies three miles north of Lauder, on Leader Haughs where the Cleekhimin Burn joins the Leader. Ask for the laird, Dand Hoppringle.' Could this be the Cleekhimin Burn?

On the far side of the stream, was a scatter of buildings. As soon as I heard the cows being called in for the milking, I waded across and headed for what looked like the main house. Dogs raced

181

towards me, barking, but were called off by a tall spade-bearded man with a fine brow, who emerged from the doorway. As we approached each other, I suddenly realized the disreputable figure I must cut — unwashed, with a week's growth on my cheeks, and filthy worn clothing. A strange feeling of unreality came over me. I felt that at any moment, the hillside, the purling stream, the line of plodding cows — all would dissolve like the vapour swirling on the haughs as the sun's rays touched the dew.

The other was the first to break the silence. "Man — ye've come a sair gait," he commented drily.

"Aye — the roads is gey clarty."

"Aweel, come awa ben, ye'll be fair wabbit."

In a tub of hot water in Mrs Hoppringle's kitchen, I scrubbed away the grime of that horrible pit prison in Hailes Castle, and of my Pictish earth-house. Then I was put into a box-bed where I slept the clock round. Next morning shaved, dressed in fresh clothes supplied by my host, I felt almost like a new man.

Not for long, however. After breakfast, Hoppringle whistled up his dogs and asked me if I would walk with him round the policies.

He did not beat about the bush. "They've tane Mossman's servin lass," he announced.

My heart seemed to turn to ice. I stopped in my tracks. "Jessie?" I asked stupidly, then. "How?"

"Haud up, lad," said Hoppringle kindly, taking me by the shoulder. He handed me a flask containing some cordial, which steadied me a bit. Then he looked at me with shrewd compassion. "Ye were close? Aye — Ah sud hae jaloused ye micht be. Gude kens wha pit the finger on her." He looked at me searchingly. "Syne thon stramash at Hailes Castle, a Lothian's been bumman like a bees' byke; it's no fur want o speirin ye've no been tane. Thon Bothwell's an ill chiel tae cross, an the airm o the Privy Cooncil's gey lang. It's cauld comfort nae doot, but seemingly she hasna telt them ocht, fur yon wily Mossman himsel's a free man yet."

It occurred to me, inconsequently, that to be telling me this Hoppringle must know something of my background and track record as a spy, also that the intelligence system which he was able

182

to tap must be highly efficient. Such irrelevant speculation was probably my mind supplying its own anodyne against the unbearable truth. I felt a curious numbness, a light-headedness almost, as I asked my next question; "Have they killed her?"

Hoppringle shook his head. Then, "Ah'm no sae sure it wadna hae been best gin they had."

Then I knew, and the knowledge was like the touch of cold fingers on my spine. With awful clarity, I recalled Barbara's prophecy, about fire and steel and a bonny face that changed — unspeakably.

"The leper house?" I whispered.

"Aye lad," Hoppringle confirmed gently, adding, "It'll no hae touched her, yet. Perhaps it niver will." But I knew with a chill certainty, that it would. And it was my fault. And Mossman's fault, and Ascham's, and ... But where did the chain end? I thought how, after my destruction of the Porcupine, my trail must have been traced back to Edinburgh, and my relationship with Jessie discovered. Eyes — keen and hostile, that had noted me with Jessie, may also have spotted me with Helen in her guise of Wattie. The connection would have been made, then they would have moved in ...

"Ah'll leave ye awhile, lad," murmured Hoppringle, and withdrew.

Was there no end to it? I wondered dully. How much pain could the heart endure and not break? At last, the healing tears came, and by Leader Haughs I wept my sorrow for my poor lost love.

There is little more to tell. The following day, Hoppringle provided me with a pack of rations and money, then took me up into the hills to the headwaters of the Eden Burn, where we parted. Here I lay till nightfall, when I followed the Eden down into the Merse, to its confluence with Tweed. I followed the Tweed upstream until, just as dawn was breaking, the battlements of Wark Castle broke the skyline on the south side. Making a bundle of my clothes, I swam across to the far bank — into England.

From Wark, I was passed on to William, Lord Eure, Warden of the English East March (and father of Ralph Eure killed at Ancrum,

183

where the whole business had started). With an escort and remounts supplied by Lord Eure, I was in London in five days. My meeting with Ascham was strained; I knew he was an instrument in the service of the State, as I had been in his, and I bore him no ill-will. Nevertheless, my nerves shrieked in his presence. Sensing this, he wisely left me alone during the two days it took me to write my report, to be delivered to Gardiner. Perhaps one day, when I am myself again, we will have that promised archery match ...

The King was generous; I have taken rooms in Chelsea, and can live in reasonable comfort while I make my plans for the future. I do not think I will go back to Cambridge, to finish the course for my Master's degree; that, somehow, is a phase that belongs to the past. I may return home to Ely and help my father in his business. Or I may travel.

Meanwhile, I think of my three loves in the North; one dead by my own hand, one waiting out a living death, and the third — wild and free, as the wind that blows on Lammermuir. If our King's great plan should succeed, and England and Scotland become one, I may leave the world behind me and go and seek my Barbara, to live with the gypsies among the hills and heather.

Well, that's it then — the tale of how Wainwright found and slew the Porcupine (shades of Perseus and the Gorgon?) and his adventures on the way ...

...and soe trustinge untoe the benignitie of your gentil acceptaunce whosoever shall hap to reade these wordes of myn I shall take my leave of you; Vale.

Oute of the House of Sir Robert Hastynges Knyght in Chelsea this 15th of December and in the yere of oure Lord God 1545.

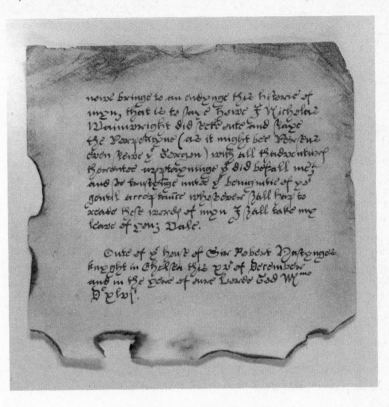

Transcription of the last page of
Nicholas Wainwright's M.S.

185

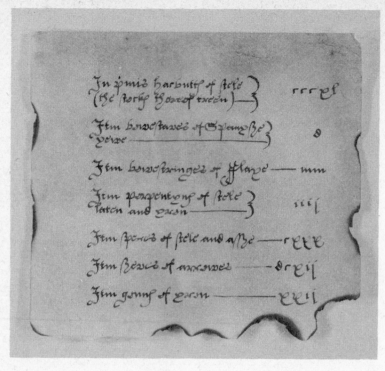

Transcription of part of an Account of military stores.

In p(r)imis hacbuttes of stele)
(the stockes thereof treen[1])   cccxl

It(e)m bowestaves of Spanyshe)
yewe ——————————)   d

It(e) bowestringes of Flaxe —————————————mm

It(e)m porpentynes of stele)
laten[2] and yron ————)   ....
                                           iiii

It(e)m speres of stele and asshe————————————— cxxx

It(e)m sheves of arrowes—————————————— dcxii

[1] i.e. tree-en — wooden.
[2] 'laten' (latten) was a kind of brass.

186

APPENDICES

1. Historical Note

I can find no direct allusions to the Porcupine (Wainwright spells it variously Portentine, Porpentyne, etc.) in contemporary documents* — which suggests that Wainwright performed his mission with commendable thoroughness. There are however certain pieces of indirect evidence which seem to me significant and which suggest that political and military leaders knew more than they cared to let on, but for reasons of national security were keeping it 'under wraps'. I have drawn up this evidence as follows:

i. Monastery used as Secret Weapons base?

Why was Markle — an ostensibly innocuous 'priests' town', burned by Edward Seymour Duke of Somerset, when he invaded Scotland in 1547? For want of any other reason, I can only conclude that it was in punishment for some offence about which History remains silent. In the light of what Wainwright has to say however, Somerset's motive becomes immediately clear — to ensure the total eradication of any Porcupine-related activity which may have survived Wainwright's mission.

N.B.

In some respects the 1547 invasion was a repeat performance in the reverse direction, of Seymour's raid of 1544 when, as Earl of Hertford, he burned Edinburgh and Leith then beat up most of the settlements in his path, en route to rejoin his fleet at Berwick. Patten's *Expedition* — a remarkable journal written by a war correspondent who accompanied Somerset's army, is an invaluable source for the 1547 invasion. It forms a useful complement to Wainwright's observations of the area, which were made barely a year after the raid of 1544.

ii. 'Nothing to Declare' at Fawside?

Why should the inhabitants of Fawside Castle have — quite needlessly and without provocation — shot at Somerset's army throughout the Battle of Pinkie (10th September 1547), thus courting certain disaster if the English should win? Patten puts it neatly. 'There was upon this Fauxside Brae a little Castle which was very busy all the time of the battle as any of our men came nigh it, to shoot at them with handguns and hackbutts, little hurt did they; but as they saw their fellows in the field driven away before their faces, they plucked in their pieces like a dog his tail, and couched themselves within all mute. But by and by the house was set on fire; and they for their goodwill, burnt and smothered within.'†

Such incredible foolhardiness is hard to comprehend unless the inhabitants had a compelling reason for keeping the English at arm's length. Wainwright shows that just such a motive did exist; Fawside was one of a chain of arms depots which the

*see Bibliography.
†*An ambitious reconstruction project is at present restoring the burned-out shell to its pre-Pinkie state. Workmen on the site report finding, in addition to skeletons, quantities of ammunition — which tallies with what both Patten and Wainwright have to say.*

Scots had prepared in readiness for an invasion of England (to be spearheaded by the Porcupine). Patten, in his summing up of the 1547 campaign describes how, after the bulk of the army had returned home, Broughty Castle, Inchcolm — both Abbey and Island, the Castle of Milk and Home Castle (now the Hirsel) were permanently occupied and garrisoned — the very places that Hepburn enumerated as arms depots to Wainwright! As the Scots forces had been utterly smashed (13,000 killed at Pinkie alone Patten claims) and Scotland could pose no threat to England, it is hard to see how such a massive and expensive 'Fortress Scotland' policy could be justified. Unless. . .

In fact, the more one reviews Patten in the light of Wainwright, the harder it becomes to escape the conclusion that the Expedition of 1547 was a follow-through of Wainwright's mission, to ensure that the Porcupine really had been scotched and would remain so for good.

iii. The Enigma of Bothwell

How was it that Patrick Hepburn, 3rd Earl of Bothwell who masterminded the whole Porcupine project, appears to have been let off scot-free by the English? Poor old semi-blind Sir Richard Maitland, who appears positively pro-English beside Hepburn (before the latter's 'conversion' that is), and who had even entertained that Scottish Quisling George Wishart, 'got his' when the English burned his home of Lethington (used as an ammunition factory for 'The Earl of Bothwell's Tirling Pin' — the Scots name for the Porcupine). So why not Bothwell?

It is, I believe, a classic case of poacher-turned-gamekeeper. The year 1545 stands out as a great watershed in Hepburn's political life and marks a startling change in his public persona. Here is a short profile.

Pre-1545

After a stormy youth in which treasonable flirting with the English culminates in Hepburn's banishment, he returns to Scotland apparently a reformed character. With all the zeal of the converted he espouses the Nationalist cause, vigorously opposing the proposed match between the infant Mary of Scots and Prince Edward of England (which would have resulted in the unification of the two countries), mobilizes a show of force against Hertford at the beginning of the 1544 Raid, bullies the feeble Arran* into coming down against the pro-English Reforming party, and champions Cardinal Beaton, the doughty patriot leader. Sadleyr, the English envoy sourly describes Hepburn at this time as 'vain, insolent, full of folly.'

Post-1545

After the surrender to a force sent by Scotland's ally, France, of St Andrews Castle by the traitors who murdered Cardinal Beaton, Hepburn's name is discovered in a document showing that he is 'bound to England'. For this he is sent to prison, but is released after the Battle of Pinkie in 1547. Patten leaves us in no doubt as to the reason. 'This night the Scottish Governor, *when once he thought himself in some safety, with all speed caused the Earl Bothwell to be let out of prison*: which, whether he did it for the doubt he had that we would have released him, "Willed he, nilled he"; or whether he would show himself *fain to make amends*, I do not know: but this sure, rather for some cause of fear than for any good will.' (My italics.)

In other words, the Scots leaders knew that Bothwell had become the blue-eyed boy of the English and were even prepared to release this valuable pawn in an effort to placate the conquerors.

Arran's portrait in Lennoxlove (formerly Lethington) tells us more about the man than pages of writing could do.

188

A week after the battle, Patten tells us, '...came the Earl of Bothwell to my Lord's Grace, a gentleman of right comely port and stature; and hereto of right honourable and just meaning and dealing towards the King's Majesty: whom my Lord's Grace did therefore according to his degree and demerits very friendly welcome and entertain.' (Compare this description with Sadleyr's!)

What could have caused this extraordinary volte-face after 1545? Only one explanation seems to make any sense — in 1545 the English came by information that enabled them to get Bothwell over a barrel and keep him there. What was that information? It must have been something pretty compromising — to put it midly, to have turned Bothwell overnight from the sabre-rattling patriot embodying the Scottish equivalent of 'Ils ne passeront pas', into the boot-licking fellow-traveller who creeps into the English camp after Pinkie.

After reading Wainwright, the answer fairly shouts itself aloud. The English now knew that Bothwell had been the Keeper of 'Scotland's Muckle Secret' (the development of the Porcupine). They also knew from past experience the sort of man they had to deal with. A true Borderer, Patrick Hepburn was a survivor first, patriot a long way second. The English authorities realised that Hepburn, as just about the most influential of the Scottish nobles, would make the ideal stooge to promote their policies for them within the Scottish Council. So they struck a bargain. If Hepburn would agree to 'plug' the English line in Scotland, they would spare Hailes Castle when they invaded Scotland and try to protect Hepburn from the wrath of his own countrymen. This is all conjecture of course, but it explains the facts where nothing else seems to.

Both parties seem to have stuck to their side of the bargain. In 1547 Somerset passed Hailes Castle with his invading army and — in marked contrast to his destruction of Dunglass and Innerwick Castles and his treatment of Markle, conspicuously left it alone, even though 'it was kept by the (Scottish) governor's appointment, who held the Earl (of Bothwell) in prison.' (Patten) Then in 1548 we hear of Hugh Douglas of Longniddry holding the Castle for the English as Bothwell 'was favourable to their side'. The Scottish Privy Council however retaliated by instructing Lord Borthwick to procure the Castle and 'keep the samyn surlie fra our ynemies of Ingland' and not to deliver 'the said place and fortalice to Patrick Erle Bothwell nor nain uthairie of his name'.

iv. Roger Ascham — Spymaster
The official reason for Ascham's extended leave of absence from Cambridge (where he was Greek Reader at St. John's) in 1545–46, was to recover from quartan fever. This, as it transpires from Wainwright's M.S., provided impeccable cover for him to set up the 'Court of Green Ginger' (we know that he went to Yorkshire at this time, ostensibly to help his father clear up his affairs), and organise Wainwright's mission. Mission accomplished, Ascham would then of necessity have been involved for some months in secret work with Gardiner, consolidating the massive political plus which resulted from the Porcupine's destruction. It is significant that the period of Ascham's 'illness' coincides exactly with the above schedule.

I suspect that Wainswright's Report, which Ascham would have submitted to Gardiner, may have been the deciding factor in launching Somerset's Invasion of Scotland, which as I have suggested, was arguably a massive follow-up exercise to 'Operation Porcupine'.

v. Did Wishart and Knox know about the Porcupine?
At the time when Wainwright saw the above pair, Bothwell was conducting what amounted to a personal witch-hunt against George Wishart, which was to culminate in the latter's arrest by Bothwell and subsequent burning by Cardinal

Beaton. The obsessive zeal which Hepburn displayed in his harrying of the Reformer suggests that he 'had it in' for him. Why?

Purely as a matter of policy, Hepburn was anti-Protestant. (The Nationalist party identified itself with the Old Faith.) But he was not the sort of man to lose any sleep over theological differences. Surely there must have been a more compelling reason than concern for doctrinal conformity, for his unrelenting persecution of Wishart? It should be remembered that Wishart, in addition to his preaching activities, was a paid stool-pigeon of Henry VIII. (He may even have been the Wishart who in 1544 offered to become the hit-man in a plot to murder Cardinal Beaton and was accordingly awarded 007 status by Henry VIII.) Had Wishart, in the course of his snooping, discovered some evidence about the Porcupine? If so, this would explain at once Wishart's 'Wanted Man' status where Hepburn was concerned. In consigning Wishart to the flames,* Beaton must have known that he would push the Reformers 'over the edge' and seal his own doom. (He was in fact murdered in retaliation barely three months later.) Yet he did not flinch from doing so. That Wishart had become a man 'too dangerous to live' is, I suggest, the only reason so far advanced that adequately explains Beaton's conduct.

John Knox, Wishart's protegé and champion before the latter's arrest, joined Beaton's murderers in St Andrews Castle not long after they had taken it over. When the Castle fell to the French, he was sent to the galleys. (Shades of Hepburn's consigning of spies to leper-houses?) In a sermon which Knox preached to the Castle garrison shortly before they capitulated, the following significant passage occurs: 'Upon the doore of that dwellinge was ane Tirling Pin and the Ungodly rispit thereon for they wald fayne enter upon that place the name whereof is Hell and the master thereof Beelzebub prince of Darknesse.'

2. The Porcupine†

Details about how the Porcupine may have worked are described in Wainwright's M.S. both in the text and in a drawing. Technically, the world was almost ready for a 'machine-gun' in 1545: rifling, complex spring-locks, breech-loading, charges enclosed in metal cartridges, multiple-fire either by revolvers or racks of gun-barrels — all had already been invented and applied. A few well-known examples are: a German rifle by Ruhr dated 1542; two breech-loading carbines one of them dated 1537 of Henry VIII (similar to the one described by Wainwright) in the Tower of London, with iron cartridge-cases to contain the charge; a three-barrelled revolver from the Ducale Palace in Venice, c. 1540, and one with a revolving cylinder and fixed barrel as in a modern revolver, by Hans Stopler of Nuremburg —

*By this time — March 1st 1546, 'Scotland's Muckle Secret' had of course been blown, but it was probably hoped to salvage something from the wreck. It is unlikely that Bothwell had been approached with the offers of a bribe mentioned above, by this date, so he would have the strongest possible motive for wanting Wishart out of the way before he could report to his English paymasters — assuming that Wishart knew something of the Porcupine. And so would Beaton — Wishart was a dangerous destabilizing agent who must be eliminated.

†Ascham's code-name is apt. His citing to Wainwright the Porcupine's legendary ability to discharge its quills at an enemy, echoes the following passage in his then newly-published Toxophilus:

'... nature gave example of shotyng first, by the Porpentine, which doth shote his prickes, and will hitte any thinge that fightes with it...'

dated 1597 but thought to be based on models going back to at least 50 years earlier. Fulminates (necessary for detonating a cartridge by percussion in the manner that Wainwright suggests) were known at this time; the 'grey powder' which Wainwright mentions was almost certainly a fulminate.

Only two factors were missing — how to obtain a gas-tight seal at the breech, and how to detonate a breech-loading cartridge by an internal device rather than by external ignition through a touch-hole. It was the solving of these two problems and their combination with the technical developments listed above, by an unknown genius working for the Scots, that gave birth to the Porcupine. The world had to wait until the 19th century for its principles to be re-invented.

P.S.

Was Signor Benvenuto — the Porcupine's creator, a natural son of Leonardo da Vinci, as Wainwright's account suggests? It is a tantalizing speculation. However, in view of Leonardo's likely sexual proclivities (as a young man in 1476, he was accused of having sexual relations with one Jacopo Saltarelli), this seems unlikely. But there is no reason, chronologically, why Benvenuto should not have known or been trained by Leonardo. If, for the sake of argument, one assumes that Benvenuto was a man in his forties when Wainwright saw him, he would have been in his teens or early twenties when Leonardo died in 1519.

Leonardo's *Notebooks* contain several sketches of projected multiple-fire guns, one of which shows an elevating mechanism similar to the one in Wainwright's drawing of the Porcupine. It is not impossible to imagine a gifted protegé of Leonardo absorbing and further developing such ideas.

3. The Map

Considering the very basic technical aids at Wainwright's disposal, his map is surprisingly accurate, and can I think, stand comparison with the work of professional 16th century cartographers like Lily, Saxton and Norden. It is admittedly a fair copy of the rough map he made ad hoc on his travels, drawn at leisure when he may have had access to other maps for comparison, but still based on information garnered 'in the field'.

The ship embellishment is interesting. The details are quite realistic (except that he makes his flag fly into the wind!), suggesting that it could well be drawn from his personal memories of the Sir Bedivere. He shows clearly the open gun-ports close to the waterline — something that he refers to in the text, and which may well have caused her sinking. An interesting parallel to the Mary Rose which went down less than three months later.

4. Some Places mentioned in the M.S.

1. Hailes Castle

Since Wainwright's time the garderobe drain in the pit prison must have been made steeper (presumably in the interests of hygiene), as the present drain commands a view only of a built-up section of bank. The present haugh below the Castle's north face, is a modern reconstruction of the one that Wainwright looked down on. It was created by backfilling from a wall built out into the Tyne to prevent the river undercutting the rock on which the Castle stands. (Presumably the original haugh was eroded away by the Tyne which here flows swiftly through a defile.)

From Wainwright's account, the damage to the chapel caused by the destruction of the Porcupine, must have been considerable — indeed the marks of the fire he caused are still clearly visible. Contemporary records maintain an eloquent silence about this occurrence — an omission entirely consistent with the authorities' 'cover-up' of the whole Porcupine episode.

In Wainwright's day the main road ran past Hailes Castle, instead of climbing over Pencraik Hill as the A.1. does now.

ii. East Linton
In 1545 it was 'Lynton' without the 'East'. The following features mentioned by Wainwright, can still be seen.

Linton Bridge — a solid stone affair of two arches, built c. 1520 and mentioned in Patten's *Expedition*. *Prestonkirk* — then called 'the Haugh'; of the Kirk that Wainwright knew, only the 13th century chancel remains, the rest being rebuilding of the 17th and 18th centuries.

Preston Mill — somewhat enlarged and reconstructed since Wainwright's time, but the kiln (15th century) probably looked then just as it does now. *Phantassie Doocot* — a massive 16th century structure, probably designed by someone who had been in France; the sloping roof gives pigeons a sheltered southern exposure — a feature common among colombiers of Southern France, to give protection from the mistral.

iii. Markle
Only a few fragments remain of this once fair-sized monastery and township about which very little is known. Wainwright's comments are therefore a welcome supplement to our scanty knowledge of the place.

iv. St. Mary's Church, Haddington
A vast cruciform church mainly of the 14th century, often referred to as the 'Lamp of Lothian' although this name actually refers to the Abbey. A few years after Wainwright saw it, the English carried out their threat to remove the roof. For over four centuries much of it stood in a ruined state; within the last few years it has been splendidly restored to something like its original glory.

v. St. Mary's Abbey, near Haddington
Three years after Wainwright's visit, the Scots Parliament met here (Wainwright's amorous Prioress, Elizabeth Hepburn acting as hostess) and decided to send the infant Mary to France. The Abbey buildings are wholly gone but the fine old bridge across the Tyne survives exactly as it was when Wainwright crossed it.

vi. Traprain Law
A Pictish souterrain or earth-house was discovered on the western slopes of the Law (known as Dunpender in Wainwright's time) by the well-known author Nigel Tranter. It would be exciting if the similar structure described by Wainwright were to be found, complete with the Porcupine's 'quills' which he left there.

5. The Manuscript

The bundle consists of several hundred leaves of strong paper, only, the work of a single scribe. The script is a bold Secretary Hand (a cursive form of Gothic that was the everyday hand of the 16th century.) Apart from being rather grimy and in parts mildewed, the M.S. is in good condition and the leaves appear to be in the correct order with none missing.

Despite diligent search at the P.R.O., Wainwright's Report which was passed on to Gardiner, has not so far been found.

R.L.

BIBLIOGRAPHY

In addition to consulting William Patten's *Expedition into Scotland*, John Knox's *History of the Reformation in Scotland* and Lindsay of Pitscottie's *Historie and Cronicles of Scotland*, I have searched the following for information concerning the Porcupine, in the sections relating to 1545 and the years immediately preceding and following.

Accounts of the Lord High Treasurer of Scotland, 1473–1566.

Acts of the Lords of Council in Public Affairs, 1501–1554.

Acts of the Parliaments of Scotland.

Calendar of State Papers relating to Scotland, (Scottish Series).

The Hamilton Papers, 1532–1590.

Henry VIII, Letters and Papers, Foreign and Domestic.

Register of the Privy Council of Scotland.